MW00911098

A Collection of Tales

A Short Selection of Spiritualy Inspired Stories

Contents

Autumn Leaves:
An Old West Buddhist Tale

List of Characters

Daniel O' Maley - hero
Seamus Cleary - villain
James O' Fallon - friend
Michael and Patrick - friends of the road

Introduction.

After some thought, I believe it best to add a short
introduction to this book. At first I thought it may
be best to leave the readers up to their own devises
in regards to interpreting the deeper meaning under
the sparse text. It is an Old West story which
follows along the foundation of Buddhist philosophy
as a chapter structure. This is more than mean
literary devise, I hope the reader thinks of how the
particular Buddhist teachings change how the text
can be interpreted. While I think it best to allow the
reader the opportunity to interpret between the lines,
I though it fair to at least tell him he would have to
do so. Let me say that there are "holes" so to speak,
throughout the story. These spaces, left deliberately,
allow the reader to interpret the story according to
his or her own notions. This book is intended mostly
as an invitation to thought. It does not attempt to
state in clear terms what is right, and what is wrong,
but merely to spark important debate within the
mind of the readers. Along those lines, it is best if
the reader pace himself or herself throughout
reading in order to allow time to contemplate what
might, or might not fill the many open spaces.

While I attempted to be historically accurate, in my
portrayal of a fictional tale within a historical

context, I again trusted the good judgement of the readers and ask that they research what I've said. I assume that such a story may very well have occurred, but did not necessarily do so in the way I've written.

The First Noble Truth
Life is Suffering

West Donegal Eire, 1873 Autumn

"Daniel! Daniel! What are you doing lad?" Shouted the barman. A young man 21 years of age stood stiff as a board staring hard into the eyes of Seamus Cleary, the village's best known rake and notorious bare-knuckle brawler. Seamus was a man of many characteristics and attributes but patience with someone in his way is not one of them. "But the man is nothing more than a common criminal, he's cheating my mother out of her hard-earned money!" Yes, and indeed he was, the poor old Mrs. O'Maley was up to her eyeballs in arrears of over-inflated rent, not to mention all the ridiculous service charges her landlord had charged her and the fictitious taxes she owed the county which Cleary swore up and down that she would be in big trouble if she did not pay. Her neighbors and even the village priest urged her to employ a solicitor but she would have none of it.

" How can you stand this lazy thief!" The young man said as he turned and landed a solid punch right on the nose of Seamus. His nose bent in, almost comically as if in slow motion. Blood began flowing from it, but of course in reality the nose its self is not much of a target. The brain and bones of the face are the real targets, and hits to them create much more shock and potentially deadly damage than to any other part of the body. However the shock value was there, both for the victim and the observers. Seamus, not a small man by any means, after a short moment recovered and took a firm hold of Daniel O'Maley. "You no-good rag-a-muffin you know full and well that those charges are good and honest payment to an honest business man!" He yelled as he gripped Daniel so hard as to cause great pain and bruise the young man's arms and shoulders. He turned Daniel around, pushed him into a nearby table, then regained his grip, this time by the shoulder and top of his trousers and shoved him outside the pub into the steady rain of the dark night. Daniel was lucky that Seamus did not feel like putting out more punishment, but with all those people watching he did not feel comfortable doing so. Daniel fell hard on the cold clammy stones of the road outside, struggling to regain his feet in the wet conditions, slipping and stumbling like a drunk man trying to get on his feet. "I'll have my justice Seamus !" He screamed. "Just wait. Every man gets his justice in the end!" The old men in the corner of the pub grew silent, quickly took a last quaff of their pints of porter and slipped out as quietly as they could. The bar man stepped back from the old sawed short fowling piece he kept under the bar, and Seamus returned to his table to recover from the incident. He drank his pint now slowly, in sips, mortified by the brazen spunk of the young man. The night ran on slowly from that point, Seamus occasional taking a sip, staring off into the corner, the pub all but empty, his clotting nose still dripping. While most had no problem with him, there were always those who see injustice as injustice and wish to stamp it out the best they can.

Seamus was a ruthless and rough man no doubt. His personality and motives base and unfeeling. However the townspeople who rented from him needed his services, for no one else in town rented out property. He provided them the opportunity to live somewhere and carry on with their lives. No one else did that. It was simply a shame that the only landlord in town for such properties was a ruthless cutthroat. But the nature of life sometimes is that those that have the opportunity to gain from others take it. It seems sometimes inevitable that there is some component of evil in all situations. Regardless of how good a community is, of how upstanding and respectable, there is always someone or something that flies in the face of all that is good.

Daniel limped down the narrow road that lead out to the main street. It was getting dark and the way was just lit by a few street lights and residences'

windows. His good friend James O'fallon saw him as he rode by on his way back home from the parish church. "Lord! Man what's happened to you?" He inquired in his Dublin accent. "Not after that rotten Seamus Cleary again are you? I know it's a rotten lot, but the fact of the matter is you're going about it all wrong, man. The best way is to have someone help you, you know? It's not a one man job. You need to have someone who knows about these matters look into it." Daniel sighed and looked a bit down trodden, he replied. "I do appreciate it James, but you know in our situation we just can't afford a good solicitor and in fact I don't know that anyone in town would be willing to fight him. Anything other than that I don't quite know, might you be referring to something
outside the law?" "No." Replied James sharply then said slightly quieter, "I don't think that would be the best thing to do. The matter is that it is a very difficult sort of thing, he is a well-entrenched man in our local affairs you know. He is not an entirely evil man either, it is just he is a business man and doesn't mind a little dishonestly if it pays for him.
Sometimes life is just not perfect, it is not what it should, or could, or might be. It is imperfect and inherently has some aspects of unpleasantness which simply can't be fixed." "That's quite a mouthful brother." Daniel replied as he looked down the road

in the general direction of his home. "I'll give you a ride home Daniel." James said and he helped him on the back of the horse.

It was fairly cold and damp even though the flowers were still blooming a bit. It was Autumn, but not too cold for a few later blooms. The light drizzle that now came down made it difficult to see and made the lights of the village shine in a way that looked fuzzy to the eye. Even though it was relatively early it felt quite late as if a long day had been spent. The scene would be quite beautiful if they both were not completely soaked through at this point. The horse's hooves made a pleasant but lonely sound as they passed the various businesses along the main street of the village. The blacksmith's house was highly lighted and the silhouette of the man sitting down to some reading could be seen on the drapes in his front room.

Daniel almost went directly to bed just saying a brief "hello" to his mother as he walked in. The small house was in fairly bad shape and in need of some tiles on the roof, a bit of paint and plaster in most of the rooms. It was a major problem since the late Mr. O'Maley had been lost at sea. He was not a great man, fairly faithful and good to his family, but he was not all that bright. As he was generally far from

home he could not look into things. He knew that Seamus Cleary was not the best of people, but under the circumstances they could not really buy a house of their own. Of course after the old man passed on the ruthless landlord took all freedoms imaginable and so they came to be in the state they were. Clearly was such a prominent landlord and well involved in the community that it was just taken for granted that he would take advantage when he could. After all, most villages do have their share of those who are less scrupulous
than most, and often they are part of the business community.

The O'Maleys had themselves in a situation which is not all that uncommon, and just seemed to fester, not really getting any better or worse. It was all a matter of how things developed over time. James and others had thought of how a simple bit of legal work with a solicitor or some government official might clean up the situation. They could clear up that or even in fact the many slight advantages the land lord took with many people throughout the area, it was just that no one ever took the initiative to do something about it. There obviously were solicitors around, maybe not many in the village its self but they were to be had, likewise Mrs. O'Maley or her son could easily look into doing something;

but nothing ever happened. One thing led to another and since no one wanted to do anything about it, nothing was done.

"So what is the wage of sin? Is it damnation, death, earthy or hellish suffering? What I ask you dear parishioners?" The parish priest asked, as he stared out into the provincial church looking, as it would seem directly into the eyes of each and every person gathered there. "The wage of sin is to live in a constant state of suffering in this life and the next, forever. This is what the bible tells us. Those who seek out earthly pleasures will surely find themselves tied to them as an ox to the plough. A life of sin is born to a death of hellish suffering and burning fire for all eternity. What can be done about it? We must repent and live our lives as good moral people standing up to the evil that entertains us and asks for our attention at every turn. We must choose to live the moral life for the sake of the next one." James O'Fallon leaned up to Daniel's ear from the pew behind and said "That's quite a pleasant thought for all of us isn't it?" The priest continued "For the wages of sin is death, an eternal hellish death of body AND soul." Daniel simply smiled silently and nodded. It was lightly misting outside as the first blooms of spring erupted from their buds Daniel noticed as he looked outside for a brief moment

Earthly suffering was something everyone knew regardless of whom he or she was. The O'Maleys, James, even the parish priest himself had their problems with the state of affairs at the parish. He would like to make changes, maybe not be tied down to the same rural parish for seven years at a time, but this is how it was, he took his orders. James had his problems with the brew masters with whom he worked also, but this is how it was, he the low man in the pecking order could not make managerial decisions. He was required to do his years of grunt work, cleaning, servicing equipment, moving grain and lighting the fires. He would learn the trade and with luck know the trade and be a master of it. As for the O'Maleys they happened into a bad situation due to no fault of their own. They did not know that the father would be lost at sea, nor that Cleary would be the tyrant that he was, the lack of steady employment was a sure problem though that they did not seem able to fix either on the case of Daniel or his mother.

Here they found themselves in seemingly unfix able situations.

The Second Nobel Truth
Suffering is Caused by Wanting

"Oh grief mother, what can possibly be done about it? We are in a hard position, we can struggle and try to make the best of it, yes I understand, but there are steps that could be taken to remove the burden and get ahead, to pull ourselves out of the pit of trouble we are in. So we can do something with our situation and move to something better. So we can have a better life. I know it's hard since father was lost but things will only get worse if we do nothing about it." It was early morning and the day's arguments and discussion of the landlord and what to do already had begun. The sun had hardly even made it's way an inch over the horizon. The tea was not cold yet in its pot and the bitterness of debt already filled the atmosphere; hanging and perforating the environs like a dank odor. Their faces were long and sour and the town had not yet risen and come to its daily business yet.

It was two days since he had heard the cries of damnation of the parish priest. He had thought about it some. The situation with the rent was none that he brought about on himself though. He was a victim so it would seem of circumstances. He was no sinner who had brought hell fire to himself. What explanation did Catholicism have for him?

Theirs was a hard position. They struggled against the problems but it seemed to no avail. Looking for some relief from the rents, fees, etc. of Cleary. Looking for wages, a job, something to pay it, they struggled. The problems were clear but yet for some reason the family simply continued to be mired in the mud, unable to work out some solution. Sometimes in life that is how it is. We seem to be controlled and manipulated by forces that we can not see. Like mice on the treadmill we work away seemingly to move forward, but yet we remain where we are. The path out seems clear enough, but for whatever reason we are unable to take it. All that Daniel had to do was to get rid of that awful landlord, make the whole village realize they can and must do something about it, or many an honest person, just like them will continue to mire in the mud of his dishonestly. Was there some sin he did not know about? Perhaps it was a sin of his father, or some other predecessor of whom he did not know. Still, the suffering was there and it seemed it would stay.

The early morning mist made its way down to the slow slope upon which the old house sat. The light colors of purple, yellow, and red could barely be seen as they emerged, preparing to darken this year's falling leaves. The house sat there just outside the village proper, in a very used condition, not falling down, and not anything to be proud of either. It once was a very pleasant house serving its family well, but those days are gone and now it is in the hands of a hard businessman. It sat on a slight downward slope, not a hill and not a valley. It sat in its arrears a bone of contention and discord for the O'Maleys, the landlord, and those who had any sense of justice. Discussed by James, Daniel, the mother, the village priest, and those who also under the pressure of Cleary. What could be done?

By the simple nature that some must rent to sleep, and some have the advantage to receive the rent from those sleepers, Cleary had them in his palm. He could continue to extort and control them, it would seem forever. Should they plan an uprising, a coup, a boycott? These all seemed intelligent enough solutions, but noone had yet attempted them. Why?

There can be a million things that grip people into inaction. Fear, mental torment, a general un-restfulness that stagnates the human body and mind. In the case of Cleary it could be difficult to know what the results of action against him might bring. There maybe more unrest after such an event than the stagnation of overinflated rent at the present time. There are a great number of things that people can want. Many aspire to many things which in turn causes suffering in the desiring its self. Then cause suffering in that once those things are achieved, they do not bring any lasting happiness.

"Yes I agree, we should put another bushel or so of oats in the batch and see how that works out John." James O'Fallon agreed. It was an obvious thing to say but perhaps the brew master was testing the young man to see what he would do, to see if he was management material, to see what sort of stuff he was made of. The two had been talking about it for a while after John came through the brew area's door having finished, no doubt the same or a similar conversation with Michael and Dan the other brew masters of the brewery. John was in a word, a perfectionist and could stand no weak efforts to produce the best beer and run the most profitable brewery in the region. The brewery had stood there for about one hundred and fifty years she was making a nice profit and the chance of expanding was certainly there. They produced some fine beers, and there was no reason they would not continue and do better and better. John had surely come to the conclusion that the stout would be much better with more oats in it, and indeed the other brew masters had no doubt agreed and concurred it was the thing to do. Why he was talking about it was unclear, except for the fact that he was surely testing James. The other brewers had no doubt come to the agreement that it was the thing to do. So John thought he would then ask James what he thought, assuming that he heard what was decided just seconds before outside the brew area's doors and see how James reacted. "Yes John that sounds just perfect to me. Give her a little more body that would be great. But you know it's just my opinion, whatever seems best to you, I'm sure that's best." John looked away and stepped out a little into the room the sound of his boots echoed though the vast spaces, standing quietly for a couple seconds. "Yes James, that is just fine I have no doubt it will work perfectly next time."

West Donegal Eire, 1874 Spring

They both, James and Daniel wanted something. Daniel found himself in a very unpleasant situation, all he wanted were the simple things that most folks want. He wanted to be free to go about and live his life, to have a trade and career, a house of his own, perhaps a wife, but mostly be free of the debts, the trouble, and the grief of the ensnarements of the landlord. James on the other hand wanted some things with slightly more nuances. He was an honest and involved young man. He helped the local church with charitable activities. He put the roofs on the houses of the poor, he fed those with no food, he read the bible on evenings at meetings, and he helped keep the church look clean and sharp. He too was a budding businessman. He knew the importance of order and planning to run a brewery, he knew attention to every detail, and was beginning to understand the nuances of market presence and financial management. He believed in honest hard work and judicial living. He would someday be a fine and upstanding citizen.

"Thank you very much James." Daniel said heartily, quaffing his pint. "That does the soul good." The sun was making its way steadily to the bottom of the horizon. The days were getting longer and quite pleasant. The brew was refreshing with a bit of a bite and substance. The drinking room where the brewers took to at the end of the day was becoming dark as the shadows drew longer. Daniel had stopped by to say hello to James. James just by chance had finished his work and was resting a bit. It was a fine day indeed. It was quite and restful. The brew masters were kind enough to allow James a few free pints a day and a little quite time at the end of the day to entertain friends in the private areas of the brewery. The two young men had a good deal to think about, but one more than the other. "You seem to be doing quite well James, why is that?" Daniel inquired. "Seems as if you have everything going on fairly well for yourself, you have a nice pleasant brewery in which to occupy yourself, but shame, no lady." He said, raising his voice and joking a little. "Ha!" Laughed James. "I don't know about that, the tailor's daughter seems interested in getting to know me a bit better. Don't you know? But the fact of the matter is that I don't think anything is completely settled. There's much work to be done before I can say I'm home free and all settled. There's many a pot of mash to be soured, spilt, or ruined you know. But I believe I will make a good go of it. The only problem is I don't know if it really is what I want, or can do with myself. I had to move here from Dublin when mother passed on you know, so my uncle could care for me and all. There's much more to life there you know."

Their chat had been longer than they expected. The time for light talk was over, and it was getting dark. The atmosphere did become a bit more serious. James said "It's almost dark I'll have to light a lamp. Let's just go for now." Daniel finished his pint and put the glass into the cleaning water. They stepped out into the street and the weather was nice. Slightly humid from the morning's mists, the length of the day had not burned away all the wetness, as the last specks of sunlight disappeared. "Yes Daniel, the job I think, it is good really, you know I could be much worse off, but also much better." They paused and just walked a little in silence for a while. "Nothing has happened with the rent today James." Daniel said. " It really is a big problem and I just don't know what might be done about it."

Things went on like this for about a week and then it all became clear, or at least clearer. The problem with the rent, was not just his, but his communities. He had to seek out those in the community who could help him, and see what they could accomplish with them. He went to his neighbor William Cyrus to ask him what he thought of the situation. It was clear that Daniel was in want of a better situation. After all it's not proper that a ruffian of a landlord is allowed to do as he please. It was not just a pure wanting Daniel had though. He had a desire to do well by his mother and protect her.

The old man greeted Daniel in his wistful way. His pipe dangling from his old lips. The man was now eighty two, his sons and daughters, all had gone away to this place or that to make lives for themselves, and his dear wife had passed on some five years ago. He smiled at Daniel, for he knew of Seamus Cleary. " Hello son, what brings you in this

27

dark evening?" He asked. Daniel explained that after some months of no progress with the landlord, things could not be fixed much. The old man listened and knew full well the problem the young man found himself in. He reminded him still though, for centuries the landlords had kept the lives of their tenants. It was for centuries in Europe and the British Iles the way life was. The master owned the land, and the serfs served him. Quite possibly for life. Was it his place to question things? Was he asking too much? Was he too boastful in his desire to be able to save a little money and be free of the rent?

William asked him all this and sat quietly by the fire afterward, his dog at his side. It was not clear what he meant to say, but he merely put the information in front of the boy for him to think about.

Daniel thought for a few weeks about the situation more. Of course it had been close onto two years since he lost his father and Seamus had started making life difficult. He was a grown man now, and it was high time he make a career and a life for himself though. The landlord was taking the lion's share of what his mother could earn with piece work of sewing, and his odd jobs. He was in a pit of suffering for sure, but was it a suffering that could be fixed, or was it simply the way of the world?

The Third Nobel Truth
There is a Space Free of Suffering

"So I think I'll try it then mother. Why does everything always have to be a trouble with you? Can't you just allow to give it a try?" Daniel had been discussing the idea of going off to America for several months now. Things were settled down for the most part but still no profession called him and the immediate surroundings promised no change to the situation. Now that most of the problems with the rent and Seamus were over, after the entire village had its showdown with him, things began to settle, but still Daniel looked for something he did not have.

With the help of James, the priest, and a whole gang of villagers, Cleary was finally brought to see the other side of the story. He forgave all the arrears and fees she owed and allowed her to move out of the house. It was either that or have the entire town refuse to pay any more rent, and possibly burn his own house into the ground. While he was a crafty businessman, he was no fool, and hardly wanted to have to move to another village with a gang of torch bearers running behind him.

Daniel and his mother had been talking about it, or at least he had been bringing up the topic of going to

America, and trying to get some sort of answer from her. This had been going one for a while. Just the past two weeks as things seemed settled, the idea came back to him, and it really did seem like a smart idea to start looking into it again.

Of course for decades if not centuries the Irish had been going to many distant lands to escape the conditions that plagued them. Famine, injustice, occupation, exploitation, and every other type of trouble had visited the Irish since time immemorial. Now, at the end of the 19th century things were the same, and Daniel thought he could best seek his fortune in America.

"James, what do you think of that? The idea of going out to the wilds of the United States and making a go of it?" Daniel was trying to get James to join him on his adventure. James gave his answer. "I have thought about it a good bit my friend. Honestly I've been thinking of moving to Dublin for some time. I've been here since the age of five after all, and sure to be sure there's much more a-doing there. However, at this point I know full well a man must make a living. The Brewery is boiling along just fine, and I think it's best if I stay on." Daniel was visibly disappointed in his friend's response. His face dropped, and he frowned a bit. He looked down to his boots at the bits of sand and gravel that covered the shady corner they had stepped back into. " Well James, I can understand. There's no hard feelings at all for sure." To be honest Daniel knew full well it would be a dangerous proposition to make the journey alone. He was sure not the first to have done it though.

A cool breeze blew, spring was in full swing, but the shadows under the four-story plaster and brick buildings were cool. Daniel and James stood there a few seconds, their relationship had been close. Now it would seem they had come to a turn in the road. "So what exactly will you be doing out there Daniel?" James asked. "Will you be digging gold out of the mountains, or raising cattle and the like?" Daniel answered, "I fancy myself a Buffalo Runner James." James stood a bit looking Daniel in the face for a few seconds, then looking away and up to the roofs of the adjoining buildings. "Do I understand it correctly that those are not the ones that run from the buffalo, but make them run?" "Not exactly James. It's usually better if they don't run, especially in your direction." Daniel said, his voice getting louder and joking a bit. As its sound bounced off the sides of the buildings that had closed them in. "Yes....Yes right Daniel, I suppose that is right. So you'll be an adventurer and a hunter then will you

Daniel?" "Tell you what I'll do Daniel" James
Continued. "I'll go to Dublin, and then leave you to
go across the sea. That seems like a decent enough
plan to me. It's been a good while since I've been
there."

So it was settled. The young men had a difficult time
telling their families how safe they would be, with
good reason their families were worried, but after
two weeks it was settled and they set out on
horseback. Across Ireland they traveled, seeing what
they could and enjoying the companionship that only
comes through adversity. Daniel was to start his new
life, send money back to help his mother, and make
his fortune. A Buffalo Skinner at that time did quite
nicely, making the equivalent of three-year's
merchants' salary in three months on the open
plains. The life was rugged at times, but not difficult.
The demand for the hides of the creatures was high,
and they were free for the taking.

Dublin Eire, 1874 Early Summer

The city bustled with the rushing of people and the
clip-clop of horses' hooves. People were
everywhere, talking, yelling, hurrying as if their lives
depended on it. "To be sure, to be sure it's old
Dublin isn't it Daniel?" James exclaimed. "What a

wondrous place it is. It's changed ever so much since my childhood." Daniel replied "Yes, and perhaps not all for the better." James said, in a softer voice now. "Oh to be sure, to be sure."

They had been traveling south and east for about three weeks. They were dirty, tired, and ready to start the next part of their journey. They had visited all the little towns of north Ireland, staying where they could, sometimes in fields, or in woods, others in hotels or guest houses. It was green and growing. The next part of the journey was that of separating. It would not be easy, but it was sure to happen sooner or later if they were get out of the rocky and poor landscape of Donegal.

"I can't believe we had to go clear across Eire and get farther away from America to get closer to it." Daniel said. Most passenger liners were going from the big city in those days even though the western shore was closer. "Don't worry about it Daniel. We're here now and soon you'll be on your way."

They stayed with James' relatives two days, eating pork roasts and drinking home made ales. James would miss his life-long friend. "It's good to have known you Daniel." James said the evening before his steamer was to leave. "It's been a long and beautiful life I believe we've had. Even though were scarcely over twenty." The fire was dying down and the pints were getting flat and warm by this time. James had plenty of opportunity to reacquaint himself with his long forgotten relatives. He would travel back with his cousin so as to be safer on the road. He continued. "It's been a long and wonderful life already hasn't it?" He got no response from his companion, but simply a look of agreement. The sunlight was barely noticeable, just dancing off their fourth story flat's floor. They were long summer days they had. The light jumped here and there as it was obscured by the blowing leaves and limbs of the street's trees. It was getting warmer by the day. James lit a couple candles and prepared for bed.

It was about five in the morning when they awoke. "Arise, arise, you slumbering sleepers!" Patrick, James' uncle cried. "'Tis time to wake for the long journey ahead." The flat was four bedrooms, and quite spacious for inner Dublin. The O'Fallons had done fairly well for themselves over the years. "We're awake, we're awake!" James yelled, and peered shortly into the living room. He was already dressed except for shoes. Patrick had a kettle on, and there were buns roasting by the fire. He was no cook, but he could get a spot of breakfast on for those early mornings. He was a foreman at a shipbuilding company, and it was many an early morning he had experienced. "Alright boys, we can't have Daniel missing his ship now can we?" He continued.

It wasn't long before they had their buns and tea and were out into the bustle of a Dublin morning. People were everywhere and crowding the streets. "Come now, come now." James would say, because they were constantly in danger of getting separated and Daniel may get lost in the crowds. It wasn't long before they were at the docks though, and the mighty shiny steamer stood before them. Rich and poor, immigrants a many, and rich American businessmen also lined the halls that let them out to the ships. James made sure Daniel had the few things he needed, and bid his friend goodbye, quite possibly forever. Daniel had all the cash he could muster, and some old gold pieces the family had no more use for. A bag of some clothes and a blanket were all he had in addition. As he worked his way almost to the great opening in the side of the building, past the clerks, the street vendors, and the throngs of passengers, he looked back, his dear friend waved and said "Goodbye you old bragger, don't forget to write." Daniel smiled, waved, turns back round, and the lines of people pushed him outside and out of view.

The Fourth Nobel Truth
There is a Path That Leads out of Suffering

New York, 1874 Summer

"Oh it's a wonderful place you have here for sure
Mr. Hoengart, but I want to be moving out on my
own now." Daniel had been working a few weeks at
Hoengart's saloon in the dank, dark, and stinky
confines of New York City. The passage across the
Atlantic had been peaceful and he meet a few new
friends. He stayed at a workman's house a few
blocks from the saloon, and had saved up some
money. This combined with what he had brought
was enough to get his start. A couple of young men
from Eire he meet on the ship kept in touch and they
all planned on becoming Buffalo runners. They
found some decent horses for just $50 a head, and
some Civil War surplus Sharps rifles from the Army.
They did not realize that horses were aplenty
everywhere. They wanted to be as prepared as
possible. Army surplus rifles were quite numerous in
the East as the armory got them back in cargo loads
and could be had cheap. At weekends there were
going out to Long Island and practicing their
shooting. Michael had a "big fifty". A fifty caliber
piece re-barreled from the Government's standard
calibers, and Daniel a 40 by 120. Patrick had a

Remington Rolling Block, but its heavy trigger pull discouraged the others from having any interest in it. They would have to employ some men or boys to skin out the animals, and possibly a guide to get them to the best Buffalo grounds, but other than this they were ready.

St. Louis, 1874 Autumn

"Are you fools?" The barman asked. "You'll die trying to cross into those mountains." The gang of three Irish Buffalo shooters had made their way via the new rail systems to St. Louis. Their horses found passage among any number of other animals, machinery and odd and ends in the rear of the trains. It was the gateway to the west, and the last outpost of real civilization from there to San Francisco. "Then what will we do?" Patrick asked, speaking to no one in particular, but just a general question. The barman and Patrick's friends, as well as the mix of bankers, frontiersmen, etc. around the bar all had equal call to answer it. The barman answered "You could become farmers, ranchers, hell if I know. The Southern Herd has just been emptied out. I know that. Ever since the railroad. You're going to have to push up to the mountains."

They had not thought about what had been happening, and just in the past five years. The animals of Kansas, Nebraska and such were nearly gone by last year with the railroad making it easy to salt the skins and ship them.

"So we'll have to go farther to find them then?" Patrick asked. The barkeep said "I'm no Buffalo man I know that, but last I heard it's very slim, excepting higher and farther out. As of 1870 with the War over many have gone to shoot the Buffalo." The Irishmen turned toward each other mumbling. Their naivete was palpable and may cause them their livelihoods. They could not exactly pick up a newspaper or text book and read how to go about doing what they wanted. St. Louis was still considered a eastern city at that time. So perhaps they did not know everything that was happening on the frontier. Michael piped in. "I think we're best to go as far as we can and see what we can see." They agreed. They picked up a few items as their foodstuffs were running low, and boarded a train for St. Joseph. The horses again in tow.

Southern Great Plains, October 1874

The boys had gone as far as the railroad could take them to that point. They mounted the horses and struck out into the wilderness. The weather was getting colder by the day and they had to start making some money and deciding what to do with the Buffalo. They heard about a small town where some 'runners were said to stay. Somewhere in the vastness between Kansas and Nebraska. It was still the southern plains so chance of getting frost bitten and stranded in snow were slim.

After about two weeks they did find the town, if it could be called that. Farmers were there for sure, bringing in the excess of their harvests to be loaded by teamsters and brought to eastern markets. Also Buffalo runners, some rich and already retired, as well as busted gold prospectors become farmers, and some that might be called the last of the Mountain Men. It was an eclectic bunch, but the town was much nearer to the railroad than was it had taken them. The runners were on their ways back to St. Louis for a bit of civilization, and the farmers were bringing civilization to the southern plains.

The three Irish got jobs as farmhands, hunting guides, and what they could for a month and learned from the retired 'skinners what they could. It seemed there were still animals to be had, but they would have to go farther north. Daniel asked one old grizzled hunter, at least 60 years of age but a life on the plains had brought his actual age perhaps into the 80s. "So will we freeze if we go up north?" The old man didn't know what to say. He thought for a moment before replying. "I've never been up that way to be honest. But I know those mountains are cold. It's hard to say if you'll find any Buffalo at all. We done cleared out all the close-by ones 'round here. I guess cold is what you think it cold. Some stay out year round if they can stand it. The skins are best in mid-winter you know. Those summer skins aren't hardly worth havein' but with all the mad rush about it, some'll go out and shoot Buffalo any ol' time."

The boys hadn't even thought about how the coats get thicker in the winter. For all that planning, they hadn't planned enough. The old man continued. "It's freezing work for sure, I'd say it's best to go out in winter, seeing as how you'll have lest competition, and better skins to get. But 'course freezing of one's fingers is always a concern."

Southern Great Plains, Christmas 1874

The boys had taken up the true 'Skinners life. They

44

were living on and off with some of the friendly
Native tribes. Sometimes still they could make some
cash by guiding rich New Yorkers on hunting trips,
and by selling the game they shot. At this time the
West, Up West, Out West, or even Way Out West
were all used to describe the new territories. It was
becoming somewhat exotic to have vast open places.
Those rich from the Gilded Age, from big cities
made it out far on occasion to see it before it
disappeared forever.

Michael had taken quite nicely to some of the native
ladies. Daniel was scout, hunter, and occasional
Buffalo Hunter, living mostly in towns, but also
getting an idea of where the railroad ran and where
it did not. Patrick acted as an interpreter for both
Government and private citizens wanting to see the
West. Freezing was a concern for sure. As they
considered their main plan, and also it became a
concern that the bison herds were indeed becoming
scarce. It would seem though that it was part of the
life. The few Buffalo Shooters they did find did not
take kindly to having others in the area. It was a
wide and expansive job. They would have to ride for
days to find a valley occupied by buffalo, but not
anyone else. They did shoot a few that winter, but
realized that if they were to be professionals they
would have to endure many more hardships, and a

much rougher climate.

Northern Great Plains, 1875 Late Autumn

Daniel heard a huge boom from over the hill. A short pause, and then another came. Boom, pause, boom, boom it rang out. It was a large rifle. The sound echoed over the vast, cold, dry landscape. He figured his Sioux friends had led him correctly. He approached slowly, being aware of the wind, in which direction it blew was important. He would wait till it was blowing directly into his face then move the horse in closer. It was Michael all right. The "big fifty" banged away. It was not a long-distance gun, but it packed a lot of power. Michael saw the approach but wasn't sure what to make of it. Daniel left the horse behind, tying a fifty-pound bag of ammunition to the horse's lead and left her about two hundred yards away. The weather was cool, but not too cool. Luckily the wind was not too strong. Daniel crept on his belly to come beside Michael and his old friend recognized him. Unwilling to scare the herd away, Michael couldn't think of any reason to deter the stranger. Nor could he think of anyone strange or crazy enough to come visit a stranger in the middle of no-where.

They both began shooting now, the herd ambling

here and there slowly. As an animal would get wind of them, or start to stray they would shoot it. They would have to scuffle, crawl, or move slowly, hunched over to keep the herd in sight, and the many skinners Michael employed would be left to do the work. After about three hours all the animals were dead.

"Where is Patrick these days?" Daniel asked Michael, swiping the dirty black powder from his hands and off his cleaning rod. "Up West, far away, almost into the mountains I believe. Sure there are bison here, you see me shooting them, but they are getting scarce." He had lost part of his accent, and was sounding more Indian and American. "Why so far Michael?" The weather and exposure had already taken a toll on Michael, he looked a good five years older than when his friend had seen him last. "I believe he likes it there, it is more interesting than these plains." Daniel stopped and just looked a bit out into the vastness of it all. He said after awhile. "So would you like to go see him?" Michael replied. "Yes I think we may very well do that. In fact may have to as things go on."

They went further on, up almost to Canada. Patrick had taken a native wife, and was living among the Indians all year-round. While he and hundreds of

47

others were helping destroy the herds, and consequently the native way of life, the tribes were still willing to take in a kind stranger, especially if he helped them fight their competing tribes. The three young men spent the next fifteen years between St. Louis, New York, and the Plains. Finally after all the years of work, they were quite rich, and the buffalo all but gone in 1885. Civilization had come to the plains, and a chapter of history closed. They closed up their lives in the wilds of America. Patrick settled in Chicago, Michael went back to County Claire, and Daniel to San Francisco. All the while Daniel keeping in touch with his mother, sending her a bit of money now and them, and writing his dear friend James.

Daniel had solved his job problem and his mother's rent problems. It was now time for the next stage of his life. He had found a life and freedom for himself, and James wrote him to say he was doing well with his three children as well.

San Francisco, 1889 Autumn

Daniel was married himself by now. He married the daughter of a rich American railroad man. The railroads were forced now to be good corporate citizens and stop taking advantage of their power.

They had connected the country, and no longer crushed down on land owners. No longer did they transport loads of Buffalo hides to the East, nor the supposed car loads of gold from California.

He had taken to walking out by the ocean, taking in the crisp air and thinking a good bit. He taught English at a local college to take up some of his time. He taught proper English not that garble most Americans speak. He had his run with despair, suffering, then found his place, and his path. He was happy, for the most part, but had deep regret for the occupation that had made him so rich, and the Indian so poor. Not only the Indian, but the whole country and the whole world. He could not help but think he had chosen the WRONG path, the wrong livelihood, the wrong actions, and the wrong life. It was easy money for sure and it seemed like the Government encouraged the activity. Somehow, he just felt it lead him wrong. There were plenty of other things he could have done. The West was a land of opportunity, but it did not offer all the opportunities one might want. He had all the trappings of a full life, and had just begun to enter the Autumn of his life. He might go back to Eire yet, just to see. He had the money, but he lacked the value of LIFE.

Still, he was not too sentimental a man. He knew the West from first-hand experience. He had lived the immigrant's life, and made of it what he could. He realized that if he could turn the clock back he would have, but he could not. He decided the Autumn of his life would be better than the Summer, and now he would take a different path.

Up West
An Old West Buddhist Tale

List of Characters

Captain William S. Danniger our hero. A man in his fifties who fought in the Civil War and now is an old retired cattleman.

Jenny, Captain Danniger's daughter.

Rebecca Danniger, Captain. Danniger's wife

Weeping Wolf, The Captain's Native Lover

Schantinger, The Captain's friend

The captain is a man who has it all, and yet has nothing. He is fighting age, but also the coming of civilization to the West. He is unsettled because he is constantly looking for more things to concur and more property. He cannot find a husband for his daughter.

The First Noble Truth
Life is Suffering

1881 Montana Territory USA
On the Ranch

"It's OK, it's OK Canso, don't worry about those mavericks." Captain Danniger said. "We can't always get everyone after all." The old cattleman and his hired Mestizo cowboy were out on the periphery of the thousand-acre ranch. It was getting cold and the sun was quickly making its way behind the mountains. The Captain was wearing a checked woolen shirt over his striped one, and his favourite hat. The hat had been with him five years, but from the look of it, it could have been twenty-five. It had a high crown that was creased to a valley down the middle of his head, and was a buckskin colour with many, many stains. Stains of sweat, blood, grease, and dirt told stories of danger, adventure, and hard work. His boots were worn thin, and scuffed by thorns and rocks. His companion wore a high sombrero himself, woven of fine grass, and it too, wore the stain of a thousand cattle drives. Canso's denim britches were torn and patched in a dozen places, and his brown face showed experience and great exposure to the sun.

It was a beautiful valley, that they had settled. It was open, green in Summer, fresh in Fall and Spring. It spread out like a picture post card of the Old West. The scene was expansive and inviting with the tips of the great mountains poking up in the far left corner, the sky was wide, it changed from crystal clear to blue, to purple, red, and orange. Now the sky was an expansive blue with wisps of white clouds.

The Captain was one of the most rich and powerful men in the territory. He did not currently have much land, but money he did have. He had accumulated this fortune over the past twenty years. His home and acreage were modest, the home a plank and paint affair, with some stucco-like parts, a porch, full cellar, and fancy glass windows and shutters. He enjoyed the life he had in The West, it had brought him many pleasures. Some times after a day of hard work, He looked over the land like an alpha lion looks over his territory. Sometimes they were looking for trouble, or new developments in the territory, other times looking at the grandeur of the land, breathing it all in. The mountains shined in the sunlight, and the rivers and streams shined silver as the light bounced off them. He had horses, and cattle, and a whole range under his command. He had power and everyone knew him for miles and miles around.

It was late October and the old Captain was wondering how many more years he would be driving cattle and horses around the territory. A thousand acres isn't really much, but it was enough to meet his needs. He had already bought and sold many ranches from Texas, to Colorado, to Montana. He had been a horse soldier for the South, a telegraph man, a scout, a ranch hand, and now a cattleman. He had sent telegraphs from time to time when not in the cattle business. As a born Confederate he saw it as his moral duty to support the cause against the North's abuse of the southern states' rights. His life was old now, many a year he had seen. He was starting to reflect on life and wonder about its many beauties. Also withe the beauties came the difficulties and heartbreak of life on the frontier. The many troubles and travails had made him stronger and wiser. His face like that of his brown companion was now beginning to wrinkle, the many years of sun and wind having taken their toll. His grown daughter was still not wed and it seemed that the territory would not produce a decent bow for her. He had about six Mestizo cowboys on his place, one of which he brought from Texas, Juan was his name and he had seen The

Captain through thin and thick.

He had been on this ranch nearly ten years, though to him it seemed like five. He had made something of it. It was not an easy task, but he had the experience to make it work. He was a hard man, but not a hardened one. The past two years had been difficult on him. He was trying to get his last daughter off to be married, and trying to decide what to do with the ranch. He brought his forty years of experience with him. He knew about the West, he knew cattle, and he knew how to deal with people. He had considerable success. It was a good life he had created. He loved the cool wind out of the mountains, and the diverse topography around him. He liked to look out in the afternoon as the mountains in the distance stretching out toward heaven, and to see the sun as it showed out through the clouds as they swept by. He knew how to survive, but more than that he knew how to create a life out of what to some would seem like nothing more than barren wilderness. What he didn't know though, was how to deal with himself, and the changing world around him. The buffalo were all gone, or soon would be, though a small band did appear from time to time. It seemed he would be gone with them before too long. It was a long time since he had been back to any of his old stomping grounds; not Texas, Georgia, nor anywhere else he used to know so well. He enjoyed the family life he had created, the suppers, outings, going to church with the wife and daughter. He considered himself quite fortunate to have lived it all. He was in a sort of rut though, and not in the mood to do much about it either.

He considered himself rich, and so did many other people for that matter. He had a fine place here, and a big bank account. He had paid his dues, worked hard, and now could enjoy it. He wasn't quite ready to stop either. Things were changing though. Captain Danniger found himself in a position where he both had everything, and nothing at the same time. It was difficult for him to make heads or tails of it. He had entered his Autumn years, whether he realized it or not and the memories of war time friendships, of business rivals, the changes he had seen over a lifetime all over the country were a back drop in his mind. His life and his world were in states of constant change. While he did not realize it, life was slowing for him. He did not realize that he was doing less these days than in years past. Time and age had crept up on him.

Change is the nature of life, but he didn't like all the changes time brought with it. The influx of more settlers and the laws they brought with them all took their toils on him. It was no longer easy for a man to stake a claim and reap a life out of the land. Fences were put up, schools and county halls, and government, they all came in too. A man had to read now, and know how to figure, and know how to get along with many different neighbours, many of whom he didn't like at all. At this point in his life he knew one thing and one thing only; the cattle business, which after his time in the Army, and his time as a scout had seen him through. Now, there was much more to life than cattle. His life had made him a commander of men, a businessman, and a sort of jack of all trades, but now it seemed perhaps his skills were no longer needed. The West that he knew was quickly disappearing and the need for him was passing away like the light of a candle burned to the end of its base. It flickered now and then, waiting for the last bit of its fuel to be exhausted.

Life was hard for him, but he had his pleasures. For him, and his kind the hardships of life were normal and to be expected. While he had power and money, this time in history was a dirty, rugged, and dangerous one. Many diseases were unrecognized and misunderstood, sanitation, indoor plumbing, and paved roads were rare. Civil rights and justice could be far away and hard to grasp. Of the pleasures he

thought were truly worthwhile, he had them for a
man of his time: a good horse underneath him, a
good pipe, the gentle wind of the plains (when it was
gentle), the soft mooing of the cattle as they drove
from one place to the other; were all good enough
to spend some time thinking of, and he had learned
to enjoy them for their simple worth. Life in the
New West was not the same though. The grizzly and
the buffalo may be gone, but law, order, fences, and
more people meant their own difficulties.

" Ride high and good!" The Captain called to Canso,
as The Captain lifted his hat off his head and waved
it in the air. Canso rode away, his job of the day
done. The Captain's horse was a little startled by his
shouting and jumped a little. He patted him on the
side of the neck and said "Easy boy, easy." He
wheeled the horse around to see Canso again, and
Canso took off. Canso nudged his horse gently to
the trail and trotted off, the old Bay kicking a little
loose dirt was he went. He took off his gigantic hat,
his sombrero as they called it, turning round in the
saddle and waved to The Captain as he left, his
duster flapping behind him.

His neighbours found it quite odd that he had the
Latinos on the Ranch at all. From time to time it was
a point of discussion, many thought it Un-American

to have them. Others thought that he was within his
rights to do so. The matter was that finding reliable
help in Montana at the time was difficult, people
came and went. Life was uncertain, and a cattleman
had to make some hard decisions if he was to be
successful. The old man was to sit there awhile in
the saddle, maybe ten minutes or so looking out, the
shadows growing longer, and playing tricks on him.
He was a man of medium stature, not tall, and not
short, he had broad shoulders, and a round, broad
head. The coyotes were starting to howl, and he
thought he saw some wolves in the shadows, just on
the edge of the creek where the tree line started. The
ground and shadows took on an almost purple tint.
His horse whinnied a little and turned its head,
maybe trying to make out what was in the shadows
itself. He gave him a nudge with his boot heel and
lead her back home. He though he heard some
shuffling behind him and he urged the horse to go a
little faster, not that he would ever admit to such. It
might just be a bear not quite ready to sleep winter
away, or a wolf. The ranch hands were all in their
quarters and making supper for themselves, a meal
of chillies and beans no doubt, served piping hot,
and with much gusto and loud talking. His wife and
daughter had their own supper cooking and they
awaited his arrival. It was dusty, the Autumn rains
gone and the plains once again dry. It had been a

good day. The year's work was mostly over, and it was his privilege to relax and take a bit of time to do things. The ladies were calling. The light getting lower and lower by the second now, now nearly pitch black, after he made the half hour ride back to the house.

"Hello daughter." The Captain said as he stepped up onto the porch. She had just opened the door for him. He said it somewhat loudly, so that she was sure to hear him, just glancing at her briefly as his eyes then cast inside and where he was going. He said it loudly enough so that it was clear he was talking, but yet just shy of a holler. She could hear the reverberation of his boots underneath the boards as he took the few steps it took to open the door. She was standing coincidently near the entry, in front of a chest of drawers. She had a drawer open and was polishing some silver. She looked up at him, with a slight smirk on her face as he opened the door. She just looked at him, not really engaging him, she darted her head up shortly, then looked back down at the silver she was polishing. . It seemed more and more that she did not engage her family in anyway. She had her few friends in town that she would visit occasionally, but the childhood games she used to play around the house, and the long family outings were long over. She was a quiet child, but her mind was always ticking. While at first one might take her for a slow wit, in fact she was quit sharp. She and her father had come to understand each other fairly well over the years, but still, she was somewhat of an enigma to him.

The light flooded from inside the house to the porch and front yard for just a second, as he took hold of the opened door, exchanging pleasantries with his daughter. She replied "Hello Father. How are things today?" She seemed to have a little dust on her boots. Perhaps she had been riding. He knew she did not expect a real response. He thought she went riding and did not trouble herself to dust off her boots before starting on the polishing. That simply doesn't make sense. He tapped her on the shoulder and shuffled behind her, seeing if his wife needed any help. He himself was a bit dusty, and went to clean up quickly in the back. Jenny was a pretty young lady, but not the most beautiful. She had Teutonic features, shortish blond hair she usually kept up in a bun, pronounced, sharp cheek bones, a fairly tall stature, and strong muscles. She had a sharp look to her, and darted her head back and forth making an account of all she saw. She was a nice young lady, but a bit too forthcoming for most of the local boys.

The Captain sat down for a brief moment, the ladies had everything in check. He was tired and still a bit dusty. It was a short day, but the months before it had taken considerable energy out of him. Though he wouldn't admit it, or maybe was not even aware of it, the work was getting harder and harder for him. He exhaled loudly, commenting on the activities of the day, not that anyone was really listening. The fire was warm and welcoming. He sat a bit and enjoyed the rest for a moment in a grand stuffed chair they had brought with them, made in Philadelphia. He sat leaning back, his legs splayed out and his feet just resting on the heels of his boots. It was a long time since he could remember the three of them just sitting and enjoying what they had there. He had dragged the daughter from Texas, and the wife, long, long before that over half the country it seemed. They had the patience to stay with him though. Lucky for him, but while the wife was willing, the daughter it seemed was just there for the ride. There they were though, all three of them. They had weathered many a storm together. While things were not perfect, it had been a good life.

He reflected on what he saw that day. All within a tiny few seconds of time, but to him he was deep in thought and could have been thinking for hours. He saw the blueish purple mountains in the far distance, poking their heads up, maybe trying to see God. His old and faithful companion all full of vitality and spirit. As the sun sunk and it became dark he could see the purple shadows becoming more and more deep and more and more dark. He wondered about if they would see more mustangs the next day. The environment totally changed in fact, from morning to night. It was wide and expansive at day, but as the night approached it became closer and closer. He was lucky to have such a spread, and after what he had experienced in life, maybe lucky to still be alive. He found that many tried the West, while history may have told of the hardships, it did not always tell of the many that in fact failed. Some immigrants, disillusioned with what they had seen went back from where they came. Those were mostly the fairly well off. Those desperately poor, made life what they could of it, wherever they happened to be. So when gold failed, or ranching they became barkeeps, or doctors, or such. Many went west to seek fortunes that did not exist and he couldn't even begin to count the numbers he had seen in this situation. All this the old man thought of in those few seconds. His mind quickly came back to the present though.

It wasn't long before supper was on the table. The fire was allowed to die down a little. It was hard work. Rebecca sweated a little, perspiration was gathering around her face and on the back of her neck. The heat and the labour taking their toils on her, it was difficult not to perspire a little. Her homemade dress swayed back and forth with her quick movements. She had her hair drawn up over her head, to alleviate the perspiration, but still her efforts made it tough and the sweat came all the same. She swept back a loose bit of hair as she approached the table, tossing her head to keep it out of her face and placed a heavy bowl-like platter of stew on the table, the weight of it made a thud on the table, which reverberated through the room. It was a white ceramic vessel and was one of the few locally made things they had for the kitchen. Civilization with all its factories was still a far way off. They had simple faire, but it suited them. She started to clean herself up, stepping over to the basin, saying cheerfully, "That was hard work, toting that huge thing. Thanks for all your help." Of course her husband and daughter had not helped much. It was a common occurrence in the household, but she had become used to it. She felt it her duty to contribute to the life of the family, and this was they way she did it. In fact she didn't mind, because there wasn't much to do really. Of course the heat of the kitchen and weight of the stew did take a toll on her. Her husband and daughter left her to finish while they set the rest of the table and gathered a few things to fill out the meal.

They sat down in a few moments, Captain Danniger sat down to the utopian domestic ideal family supper of the nineteenth century. While the daughter was difficult to communicate with, and the wife was hard working, everyone was happy, at least in their own minds. The Captain had amassed a considerable amount of power and money, the wife had raised some good children, and the daughter, well, the daughter was seemingly in a world of her own, but she had no complaints. There were no big stresses to worry about, may be only the occasional wolf that stole one of the stock. It was unfortunate, but the conversation turned to the bad fence accident the Bauers had in the next county. One of the boys was chasing after a few strays. He did not realize there was a barbed wire fence in between them and himself. He charged full speed forward and ran his horse straight into the barbed wire. He was badly cut, and his wounds became infected. Proper medical care was far away and they just patched him up the best they could, and left it at that. It was about three days later they realized that they did not clean the wounds as well as they should have and that infection had set in. The quiet of the plains and mountains was nice, they could have all the quiet they needed, but when it came to needing a doctor, the distance and ruggedness of their conditions worked against them.

It was a quiet night, except for the call of the coyotes and the whispering of the wind. After the supper, Captain and the two women took to sitting in the front room, he with his pipe, the others with books. They were educated women, for women of the time, and had no problem in discussing anything with anyone. High intellectualism, or how to dress a hog, it was all the same to them; these ladies had no problem talking about any of it. "Well Captain," Rebecca said after a while, pulling down her spectacles, and dropping her book roughly from her face, down to her lap. "What are we going to do about all those wild horses over near Eggers, breaking the fences and all that other nonsense they do over there?" She said, looking at her husband over her specs, and glaring a bit. Not quite smiling, not quite staring. "We'll get rid of them eventually Rebecca." He said. His wife had trusted him to take care of so many things in the years gone by; he found it interesting that she felt a need to say anything about something now. " Me and the ponchos will get rid of them sooner or later." "That's what I'm afraid of." She replied, now smirking a little. "Later." They sat in silence a short second or two. Then he started again. "We can't just go and find them all you know. It takes time to get them and retrieve them, and all that. We want to see how many can be broken and sold. They keep on just coming in off the plains. I have no idea why." She stopped her glaring and just sat a bit; she leaned back into her seat a bit, seeming to at least be somewhat satisfied with the answer.

They settled back into their own activities and the evening passed much like any other. The Captain did think about his daughter though. She just could not find a husband, and it seemed much overdue for her to start a family of her own. Still, she was a needed hand at times, and could help them with keeping the place up when the Captain was away on business. Business took him far away sometimes, but not nearly as much as in years past. He would have to drive cattle here or there, talk business with other cattlemen, and the like. The railroads meant fewer long-distance drives for him though.

The family was happy, Jenny enjoyed the time she spent with her father, and Rebecca enjoyed the privilege but also the rustic nature of her particular lifestyle. They were a necessary part of the American experience. While their coming onto the plains meant the end of one civilization, it meant a new peace and prosperity for the nation. Directly after them though, came progress, and with it law and regulations. The Dannigers were a happy family, but one in the midst of changing times.

The cock crowed early the next day. Captain Danniger was up and making coffee before anyone else in the house was awake. He had quietly snuck out of bed, not even lifting the covers, but just moving sideways, keeping his body weight on the mattress, as he put one leg and arm on the floor at a time. His wife never had a clue he had moved. He snuck into the kitchen and rekindled the fire to make some breakfast. He looked out across the field and saw the Mestizos' lights on, it was a good three hundred yards away, and could just barely see some sombreros in the early light as they worked their ways around the buildings and into the barns. Their lights shined like a beacon in the early darkness. They were not local of course, he had brought them from Texas, and it was with some local discord and curiosity that he did so. He found them all good sound men, but the matter was that when he retired they would be forced too also. If they were to go back to Texas or not was a matter still up in the air. They could go where they pleased, but if the locals were going to allow it was another matter all together. He did not think about these things for the sake of sentimentality, but because he was a businessman. Every good businessman has a plan for the future and tries to predict what will happen in the marketplace over the next few years, if not decades. The water boiling on the stove brought his attention back inside the house and he went back to his coffee making.

The Captain went on about his day. He had a little breakfast, rode down to the cowboys' bunks, and they were off across the ranch again to wrangle in some of the wild mustangs Mrs. Danniger had been talking about, it was a fairly slow day again like the day before. The cowboys would try to sneak up on the wild horses when they could, and rope them. While it was their nature to holler and carry on while doing such, common sense got their better and they tried to be as stealthy as possible. After a few hours their hands became tired with all the roping and pulling on the great beasts.

They would have to then move on to sell the horses so rather than go back they decided to make a fire and cook up lunch there. A few rabbits and maize were enough, and the Mestizos were prepared with some cooking gear. The rabbits could be shot fairly easily. It was a good day. The wind blew in out of the mountains, but not too hard. They quickly got their rabbits dressed, and the maize in a pot with some water. It was fairly dry, and they quickly got their fire lit. After a while, they sat down with The Captain and spoke mixing Spanish and English. "Soooon Captain, soon, I think the snow will come Canso said. What then? The wind is in the mountains now, and soon will be here." For then there was no answer, and everyone just went on discussing this and that.

The Captain was able to gather up many horses and they were taken off to market. Of all his years there, he still could not believe the Indians did not pick the ones they could. Of course there were becoming fewer and fewer Indians. It was like taking something for free and getting paid to do it, simply picking up money that was laying there. He just so happened to be at the right place at the right time. Many things were like that in the Old West: Land, buffalo, even gold, could be had by those willing to pick it up.

"That's good Poco, that's good." Captain said, as he bid them farewell. The Mestizos turned their horses and trotted off, leaving the Captain and his two men. Three of the Mestizos were going off to the next town to sell the mustangs, it would be three days before they saw them again. The wild beasts didn't like it any too much, but being tied as they were they couldn't get away or run too fast if they did. The ranch hands had tied the legs of the horses in such a way that they couldn't make a full stride. The domestic horses had a calming effect on the animals, and while the mustangs did pull a little at their leads, it seemed it would not be too much trouble to bring them in. The Captain trusted the men to do the work, hired hands or not, they were fully capable of doing the job. "Well partner, let's head home." The Captain said to Juan, robustly as they turned their horses in the opposite direction and went home. His saddle bags flopped a little as he turned the horse. It was a good day, still early enough to get home before too dark.

He was covered in dirt from head to toe. His companions had been wearing the same shirts the whole week. It was Thursday and they put them on Sunday. Death and the danger of it followed them everywhere, and hospitals and modern medicine were far away both geographically and chronologically. The gear of the cowboy was uncomfortable. Heavy chaps and britches weighted him down and buckled on his body. Rain, snow, and mud were constant companions as were boredom. Coffee and tobacco helped keep them awake, but the dangers were real and constant. The Captain had many lives since he was born. Army man, scout, Indian translator, and businessman. He knew all to well that life is not always as fine and wonderful as it could be. He knew these boys that were with him knew no other life, and wondered what would become of them when he retired, if he ever did. Still, it was a fine ranch he had. Space to think, and opportunity to spend time with his daughter gave him a great life. He could remember the many hours he and she spend looking at the herds, roping, riding, and surveying the land.

Juan, Canso, and the Captain got in just about an hour after dark. The horses knew their ways back well enough they didn't need light to make it. Rebecca and Jenny had already had their supper. It was a still evening, but some rain was just starting as he got in. The harsh Montana winter would soon be upon them. "Hello, hello." He said as he came in. Jenny was reading a book, and Rebecca had gone off to make a social call at the neighbouring ranch. "How are you Jenny?" He asked, she just said "OK, how are you?" Making no mention of what he had been doing, or the fact he had been gone all day without seeing her. She hardly moved as he sat down, looking around, the dirt on his boots knocking off and onto the floor boards. "Any news?" He asked, wondering yet again about his

distant daughter. The neighbours insured him all teenagers are like that though. He couldn't remember having such troubles with any of the other children
though.

"Did you do anything important today?" He asked this time, and she just said "No", going back to her reading. He thought at least it's good she can read. Rebecca made her way back home before too long. She was in good spirits, but tired and went directly to bed. Jenny agreed to go out and do some riding with her father the next day.

Jenny and The Captain rose a little later than usual and it was nice to get out into the fresh Autumn air. The Captain opened the windows briefly right after getting up to freshen the house. The curtains blew gently in the breeze. The cowboys had little to do, and just checked the fences. Soon some would be going back to Texas to winter there. It was a rough life for most of them. The Captain kept Juan on all year, but most of them wandered from place to place finding work where they could. The Captain took Jenny up to the cliffs in the foothills of the mountains that day. It was nice to get some fresh mountain air. The streams were just starting to freeze up a little and Old Man Winter would soon be upon them. Soon they would be locked in the house by the cold and snow and it would be difficult to take an outing such as this. They looked down into the valleys behind them as the soil crumbled and small stones tripped their ways down into the stream beds below. Soon it would be a dangerous prospect to take these trails with ice and snow coming. The horses clip-clopped their ways along the rocky paths, and past the green growth as they went. The Captain would look up and around every once-in-a-while and see the slowing growth of the vegetation, and see where Jenny was, so she did not get too far behind. After a couple hours it seemed like a good stopping point and he turned and waited awhile. "Well Jenny." He said before too long. "How do you like the view?" She looked out herself now, for a good long time, her long straight blond hair whipping a little in the wind. She replied "It's beautiful, some of God's creation we have here to see isn't it?" He turned his horse round to get a better look himself. They sat there a good seven minutes, just looking. When you're doing something seven minutes isn't all that long a time, but when you are siting and breathing in the beauty of God's creation, seven minutes gives you plenty of time to really get an idea of what it is all about. So they sat there seven minutes and soaked it all in, seeing what majesty it really was. The streams and valleys below shown all sorts of colours: purples, and violets, and greens and browns, along with the sparkling whites of the water.

They started up again for another twenty minutes, and the trails began to run out. The wind started to whip considerably violently as they got higher and higher into the mountains, and it seemed prudent to head back. It threw the Captain's hat brim back over his face, and then slapped it down into his face, whistling through the trees as it escaped the peaks above them. He was a little shocked at the brim slapped him, and then his hat nearly leap of his head. The horses whinnied with concern and acted unsettled. They were almost in the territory of the mules and goats at this point. The lush greens and blues of the foothills had been left below them and they were starting to see mostly scruffy bushes. They decided it was time to go back. They eased the horses around and led them gently back down the mountain.

It was a good day, a pleasant day, and a day that not everybody in this world gets to enjoy. He sat there on his steed a short while. The cold of the mountains had his rheumatism acting up, his old bones felt stiff and uncomfortable. The old man knew full well how

lucky he was to have the opportunity, and he had
worked a long time to get there. It was not that
when back in Texas that he had thought about the
pleasure it might bring to be Up West, but rather, at
the time it was simply a new opportunity he had to
explore. Now, that he sat there, next to the ranch he
had built, his daughter by his side, he realized the
beauty of the place, and the extrodinary time in
history that they found themselves. It was a
changing place though, and the Old West would
soon be a thing of the past. The mountain men were
almost an extinct species by the time he was ten
years old. He knew his time too would soon be up.
The lone cattleman of the plains, moving herds
almost a thousand miles at a time, the open plains
too would soon be a thing of the past, but for now
he was happy.

They let the horses rest and take a good long drink
after coming off the mountains. The poor old
animals had some strain on the way back down.
They drank deeply and rested a few moments
without their saddles on. The Captain and daughter
crouched down themselves and drank what was left
from their canteens. The return journey was an easy
stride for them, as they pushed through the grass in
its last glories of the season, high and blond
coloured, shedding its seeds for next year's

generation. It was still fairly early when they got back and had a chance to help out Rebecca with their pork supper.

Winter 1881- 1882
In Town

"Hello you! You old scudder ruff you!" The Captain yelled at his friend and long-time business partner as The Captain came in the door. "What are you up to these days?" Mr. Schantinger was a land investor and local politician that knew Captain Danniger ever since he had moved to the foothills. Schantinger had been mayor, cattleman, county clerk, and many other things. He had been one of the first locals that The Captain had befriended. He, like the Captain had been a rancher and cattleman, however Schantinger discovered early that he might be better off becoming a speculator in the western land boom. They were discussing who was moving into the territory. Fences were the norm these days, though not too long ago the Dannigers let their herds roam free, and long drives to Kansas City and the like common. Now almost every man kept his animals behind fences, and as the railways made their way into Montana, the need to drive cattle across country stopped. Schantinger was one who helped them draw the plots up, and helped divide the homesteads. The had a beer together and looked on at the cowpokes, miners and the like that occupied the tiny saloon in this tiny town of Montana. The place had bison heads and stuffed bears as well as the typical squeaky pine floors typical of the region. Danniger looked up at one of the old bison heads, its vacant brown glass eyes staring at him, and said to Schantinger "Well how about it?" He wanted to see if anyone had been buying new parcels of land, and if there may be any coming up for sale soon. He liked to keep an eye on things, seeing as how he had a position to have things run smoothly around there. Schantinger replied, after some thought, and he too looked up at the old and in fact somewhat dusty head, "There's nothing too much going on. I have sold a few ranches this year though, I mean this season. Last Spring up until now is what I mean. There are honestly not going to be too many available before too long. Some are taking to grow what they can here, cold as hell or not. There is a bit along side your place sill though. Why do you ask?" Danniger replied "Oh just like to keep an eye on things. I was thinking maybe I'd run for office or something." Schantinger had not seen his friend in some time and thought for a second he might be losing his mind. He never heard of such a thing. Danniger had a strong distaste for politics, even

81

though the fact of his position ensured that he did have to play in politics of sorts from time to time. He was a part of the Old West, the West without fences, the West of vigilante justice and of true grit. Still, things do change. "Really!" Schantinger exclaimed. "Really, you a politician? I can't believe it." Danniger replied "Not exactly, I though maybe County Clerk, or something of the kind. You know?" Danniger's companion stopped for awhile and looked down at the barman tending his glasses. "Yes... Yes, I think I could see something like that. Why do you want to mess around in something like that for though?" Schantinger could not believe the old cattleman could change his stripes. Not really at least.

Danniger remembered his early years in Texas, a man could pick himself up a piece of land and make something of it. There were no investors like Schantinger speculating on what would happen in the West. Hell, back then the East was the West. While he had grown to like old Schantinger he also hatted him, because he knew what the man represented. He represented the long, boring, process of law and the complexities of a modern economy. With the influx of people like him came the end of those like him. Those who believe a man had a right to stake out a claim and make it his own.

Winter 1881-1882
Back at the Ranch

As it became colder and the snow came they had
less opportunity to go out and do things. In fact at
times the snow would be feet thick, and would
remain for weeks on end. Rebecca started her
sewing for the winter, she still made much of their
clothing as shops were far away. While certainly
they could buy whatever they needed she felt
comfortable with doing things the old-fashioned
way, they way they did things when they were first
married. She would buy some calico or the like from
traveling salesmen as they came through, they were
rough men that made their ways that far off the
beaten path, their beaten horses or mules half
starved by the time they saw the Ranch, and
themselves half frozen to death. The occasional
Indian party accounted for leathers and furs, she
would use for coats, vests, and the like. She would
sew up a shirt, coat, skirt, or whatever they
happened to need.

"What the hell are you doing?! Why what the hell is
wrong with you damn sod busters? You're thinking
about plowing under my land you idiots." The
Captain had been out looking at his fence line and

seeing what was going one around the periphery of
his acreage. Some of the new farmers of the area
were clearing some of what looked like his land, and
he was none too happy about it. "It's not bad
enough you come digging around in that soil and
muddy up all the streams, you were going to just
plow under what's not yours." It was a disputed
piece of land that was not clearly drawn up. It was
the sort of thing that was often disputed at the Land Office.

The days of simply staking a claim and working it
were over, more and more ranchers and farmers had
to bring in the Government, be it local or federal, as
well as the Land Office, or even attorneys. It would
seem the neighbours that had just moved in did not
know exactly where the property line was, or maybe
they did and had the notion to sequester some of his
land and see what happened. They had better think
about it twice before doing that. The old man got off
his horse and ran right up to them screaming and
flaying his arms around like a half-dead chicken.

Mr. Smith, an old grizzled man, with short whiskers
and an old beaten gray felt hat spoke up. "We're
very sorry sir." He said slowly, drawing out his
vowels. "We are just out looking at the property
line." He stopped and drew out his next sentence.
"Just wanted to do some planning before the Spring.

We didn't mean any harm. We just wanted to see exactly where the property ended." Of course it was a tricky piece of land and chances would be they'd argue about it in the Spring, but Danniger was at least somewhat satisfied with the answer and cooled down a little, he lowered his arms, and stood back a little from the farmers. Smith seemed to be the patriarch, and if he said he wasn't going to start plowing Danniger's land that was good enough for him, at least until Spring. He'd have to give them another look then.

"Well, what's your name then?" Danniger asked, looking straight at the newcomers. They introduced themselves, and told him how they came to Montana to farm. He relaxed a little now, and laid his arms to his sides. He could feel himself getting his breath back, he had made the horse run a little as he approached them, and jumping off and running in their direction had got his heart pounding. He stood straightening himself a bit, putting his clothes back in order, breathing, while they made their apologies and finished introducing themselves. They were from Sweden, and Smith was not their original name. It was one they chose for themselves though, and it seemed to fit them. They seemed like decent folk, wearing their high boots, and broad brim hats. They were plain people and did not seem to be too outspoken. He liked that in people. They did not seem like the kind of people who would steal another person's land. There were three of them, the father and two sons, just looking at the property line so they could plan the plowing. He left it at that, and bid them good bye, at least until he saw them again.

It was cold, winter was fully upon them, and winter in Montana was cold. Danniger wore a pair of Long Johns, his wool hunting cap, thick wool socks, two wool shirts, and his buffalo coat. While the top of him was quite warm, his toes were quite cold. The wind was not too bad, lucky for him, and the Swedish for that matter. He could see the snow high in the mountains, covering them for most of their heigh. Snow was on the ground down below also, but just a few inches. Soon he wouldn't want to venture out for anyone or anything, except maybe to hunt. The Mestizos were all gone now, but Juan, and they might be the better for it.

Jenny kept up reading her books, and did have the occasional conversation with her parents. She liked seeing an occasional friend, but no suitors poked their heads out and announced themselves. At times she would be snowed in at a neighbouring ranch, and have to stay for days, only to return on snowshoes accompanied by her friends who would perhaps in turn be snow-bound at the Danniger's a few days. She helped The Captain with an occasional fence, and her mother with cooking, cleaning, and the like. They had no domestic servants on the Ranch, while they could use them, they were practical people and saw no need to indulge in such extravagances. It was hard work for her, when she had occasion to do it, but she enjoyed it, as it gave her something to do in the long boring hours of Winter.

The Captain had done most of his work for the year, he only needed to shelter and feed the occasional head of stock. He kept their numbers down in winter, only keeping a few for the Spring's repopulating. Having cattle survive the long winter on the Plains or mountains was a tricky prospect, as the animals were just not suited to take the conditions. He found it better to simply keep a few as warm as he could and then buy stock in the Spring. Fencing, the odd business deal, and doing some paperwork occupied his Winter. He would like to sit by the fire on occasion, with Jenny or Rebecca and just talk about they day, or what their plans were.

He experienced considerable hardships throughout his life, but he did not consider them as such. They were all just natural for the times. Cold, heat, dirt, disease, and unreliable infrastructure were just part of the picture. His times were filled with human rights violations, corrupt politicians and business people. The uncertainty of life in regards to due process, land claims, security and freedom was just part and parcel of life. He, along with almost everyone else just took it for granted. He was able to survive though, and work through the roughness of his conditions to excel, and make life a grand and wondrous thing. He could not remember the number of times farmers put up their fences to stop his herds, the times bankers and politicians had tried to put up their own obstacles to his actions. Every time he had managed to get through though, sometimes after considerable fights.

Late Winter 1881-1882

"I think I'll take up Schantinger on that offer to go out hunting, honey." The Captain said to Rebecca as they finished their chicken supper. The long whiskers of his mustache drooping down as he whipped the last bits of chicken noodles from them and laid his napkin down. He looked up at her, straightening his back against the creaky rustic oak chair. "He mentioned last week he was going to pick up a buffalo, some were spotted about fifty miles into the mountains. The Sioux were no longer living there, having been deported by the Army." His blue and red checked shirt, now faded with time on the range wrinkled a little as he moved back and forth. Christmas had come and gone, and New Year's too, still the snow was deep and it was still very boring, and the nights long. She replied it sounded like a perfectly good idea. "Yes honey, that sounds good, will you be taking Jenny with you?" Jenny now drew her attention to her parents; she had been day dreaming again. She looked at them, her dark flannel dress bringing out the bright blue of her eyes. He looked at Jenny now for just a second, as she frowned a bit. It was unlikely she would want to go. He said, looking at her now, "What do you think?" She thought for a second, and said "It's awful cold you know? Do you really think I'd want to go kill some nasty old creature and drag its poor old body back here?" Her parents went back to their conversation, changing the subject to the Indians. Whether or not it was an injustice the white man had done them. They were still a part of Montana life, but it seemed not a very big part. The Army, Government, and settlers saw to it that they moved, either on their own, or with some encouragement. If it wasn't starvation, it was disease that took the red man.

The rest of the week passed much like any other. The long nights of reading, sewing, a little saddle work, maybe some work on the house, varnishing the floor, patching the walls, or any other thing he could think of to pass the time. He helped Rebecca with what he could, and she had plenty, though there was less work, it being late in Winter. He Jenny worked with him through some Thoreau and Whitman, and did listen to some of his unending advice. They were happy to have him around. Rebecca remembered the few first weeks after they had meet, it was a grand party in Athens Georgia, he was a young budding officer, and she a blushing beauty. She remembered it drove her mad to be around him, until he finally made his intentions to court her know. The days were long gone now, but seemed like yesterday.

Then the big day arrived, old Schantinger arrived, his mule in tow. He yelled his normal obscenities and greeting as he came. He had some difficulty in getting there from town, the snow being deep as it was. Being on the main road or not, it made little difference, the old rutted path was difficult to travel. Danniger greeted him, sticking his head out the door way, grinning widely at the frustration of the old man. "Howdy, sorry to see you're having so much difficulty. I'll be out in a little." The Captain said. He gathered his old Sharps, war worn, scared stock and all, along with his gear, and headed to the barn for his horse and mule. He brought some dry corn, jerky, cooking pots, blankets, Long Johns, bear grease for his boots and saddle, and some sewing equipment in case he needed to patch up a saddle or his gloves. He had a full length buffalo robe on, and heavy gloves as well as fur mittens. He gathered all this up, and tossed it up over his shoulders, and on top of his head before walking down to the barn. They were off to the mountains.

The Ranch was located just within a day's ride from the range that lead into the Bitterroots. The bison of course went down into the valleys for winter, but a small ridge of mountains hid the main ranges that connected to the Bitterroots from the Ranch. It was in this valley behind the first range, and between it and the subsequent ranges that they were to find their animals. They went through a pass, and there before them the valley opened up, with plains and rolling hills. It was forested somewhat, and they would have to make slow progress to find the animals and not spook them.

They tied the mules and gear to some trees. "Do you think anybody will get to them?" Schantinger referred to if anyone might be about and steal the mules. The Captain looked around a little, up to his ankles in snow. The wind whipped his face bitterly. He replied "Not sure." As he looked around a bit more. "I think it's unlikely. I can't see any sign of anyone, but then again, we'd be dead if we lost our gear." They decided to take the mules a bit further, even though they did make some racket, all the packs and equipment banging on their backs. They traveled slower now, looking carefully as they went. If the mules were to start hollering they would be in trouble and the bison would run for sure though. After a couple hours it was getting late, past three-thirty, and they decided to make camp, expecting the bison to make an appearance any second.

They made a small fire and cooked up some beans and coffee. They settled into a quite conversation, trying not to disturb the game, and cups of their strong coffee. They made up their bed rolls and cleared some ground to sleep on and were laying down and surveying the valley below when a small band of bison did appear from behind some pines. It looked like there were two heifers, two adolescent males, mostly likely their calves from the Spring and then a possible two or three-year-old bull. They looked for a fair while till they could make sure those were all the animals. It was not easy, because they were very cautious. They nibbled what brush they could, and moved slowly among the trees. They were most likely looking for easier pickings, and moving further down in elevation to do so. After about ten minutes of watching them Danniger spoke up, whispering in Schantinger's ear. "Dang!" The Captain said, trying to keep his voice down, but still showing some irritation. "Too bad, doesn't look like any good choices for us. That young bull would be the best we could manage. None look prime for cooking." Schantinger replied "Why is that? Seems like any of them might make for good eating." They sat, or rather crouched, sometimes taking a seat where they could without getting their britches soaked with snow, and made further assessments of the situation. Schantinger again spoke "Do you think we'll get a second chance?" Meaning would they find any other bands in the foothills. It was going to get dark soon, and the prospect of having a carcass to attend to or, to track a wounded animal after dark is something neither of them wanted to do. So taking what they could from this band was seeming like slimmer and slimmer prospects, but Schantinger was afraid they may find no others. They watched the sun sink to the west. They shifted positions slightly, and the older of the cows looked up.

She stood for a couple seconds, smelling, and looking as best she could to see from where the sound came. The two men stopped and were totally silent for a couple seconds. The cow looked again, and was off, the rest following her. "Ah!" The Captain exclaimed, though somewhat quietly. As he watched the animals turn tail and head through the trees and down hill. Not quite at a walk, not quite a gallop, kicking snow as they went. Schantinger turned his head, getting to his feet and exclaimed "God damn it!" But, it was done, and their hopes were gone for the day. The Captain said, after a few moments, "Well, we'll have to try tomorrow, it's no great loss." Schantinger had no choice but hope that it would be in their best interest to find better prospects tomorrow. The Captain was not a wasteful man, nor was he a man to chance merely wounding an animal, or taking an animal before its prime, he said "I've always considered myself a man with direction, I guess no reason to change that now."

They tied the mules and horses at camp and walked a few hundred yards up the next hill to see what the next valley looked like. It lay before them, with a coating of snow, somewhat less deep than the previous one. Speckled with pines, it was a small sort of foot-hill valley just like the previous one. They did not see any bison, but did not expect to either. The Captain asked, "Do you think we'll find any here?" Schantinger replied "Not sure, I think we're best off just to wait and camp there for now. Nobody knows, we might get some right next to us in the morning." They went back, it was nearly dark now, the hues of twilight filling the valley, and colouring all the trees with murky shades of brown and purple. They snuck into their make-shift lean-to, and insulated themselves as well as they could with buffalo robes and oil skins.

They woke up just before dawn the next day, it was rough sleeping, but the cold combined with their tiredness made them sleep a little sounder. It was difficult to get comfortable, and the coyotes kept howling nearly all night. They would roll themselves up and bury themselves as deep as they could in the robes. The days were not too cold, just below freezing, but as midnight turned, it became bitter. They made a fast breakfast of jerky and corn pone cakes and were in the saddles within thirty minutes, the discomfort of the sleep drove them to get moving as fast as possible. The rode up to the next valley, and just to the other side of it and waited. There was buffalo sign, so they waited about two hours, pinning the time away, Schantinger puffing away at his brier pipe, and moaning and complaining every once in a while. A band of six bison came round this time, a large bull, with three cows and two young ones. "Who's who?" The Captain asked. Wondering which animal or animals might be their targets. "Big bull?" Schantinger suggested, asking "How old do you think he is?" Schantinger peered out with his spyglass to have a better look. Schantinger thought out loud, "Not sure, might be a little tough you know. Not too good eat'in." The Captain didn't say anything but just thought unfriendly thoughts about his colleague, realizing that the old bull would be stringy and tough. They sat and thought a good long time, hiding behind some scrubby pines and brush. The Captain spoke up after awhile peering from under his broad hat brim, pushing the hat back over his head and peering over the pine bush for a good look. "I think either one of those youg'uns, and that bull will be just what we need. No chance they're not weaned, especially in winter, don't think they'll miss momma, and might be good eat'in." Schantinger replied, after peering over the bushes himself, "I think we should take those two young ones, best all around, the old man will get some new babies in Spring rut with no problem." So it was decided, and they waited for a shot. They rested their rifles on what branches they could and called their shots. Captain left, Schantinger right, it seemed like forever till both animals offered open shots at the same time. The Captain signaled with a short "hiss" and they fired simultaneously. They hit their animals and they were down. The other bison got wind of them, and charged, the oldest cow leading the way. The men used the brush to their best advantage, but the animals did not care, the men were lucky enough to have the old pines around, and up they went, scampering like squirrels, Schantinger complaining all the way. They dropped rifles, and everything as they ran. The bison made their attempts and were off, just making one round on the part of the bull, and two sweeps by the old cow, their fallen comrades left behind them.

The men looked out as the animals trampled their way through the snow, and off into the woods. They wanted to make sure they were gone for good, it might not be that rare for them to come back to guard their fallen compatriots. They showed no sign of turning though, and the men came out of the trees. "God damn!" Schantinger said as he cleaned himself up, pine sap all over him. He tramped the ground as he tried to get all the twigs and debris off of him, he lost his wool cap on his journey up the tree and picked it up. He continued " Well, do you think they'll be good eat'in?" The Captain replied "yeah, sure, you old fool you wanted yourself a tough old trophy though didn't you? You should thank me for being your better judgement. That sucker would be as tough as nails. Hell, let him spread his seed." Schantinger didn't say anything but simply walked over to the animals, checking to see if they were playing dead. He knelt down and drew his knife. "The dead ones are the ones that kill you, you know!" He said. Indeed they were, for many a buffalo pretended to be dead only to jump up and gore his skinner. Schantinger leaned over and began positioning the beast, getting it on it's back, it weighted about one thousand pounds. His friend emptied the old black powder cartridge from his old war piece and came over to help his friend. It was a big job, and they had only two men to do it. They were lucky the animals did not travel once shot, and both were on fairly level ground. The men pulled and pushed the thousand pound beasts as best they could before gutting and quartering them, and wrapping the meat in the massive and heavy skins. It would soon be frozen solid, unless they got it out of the cold.

The Captain and Schantinger took about two hours to clean the animals and get them packed up. The poor night's sleep still taking a toil on them, they decided to make tracks as soon as possible. Around noon they started back on their day long journey, it would be a five to eight hour ride that day, and then they would finish up the next, and happy to make it back home. The rough sleeping outside was much more unpleasant than in the years they remembered in the past. Their old bodies could not take the roughness of the ground, or the freezing cold as they could in the past. "Why don't we just travel on?" Schantinger suggested, meaning they should travel till they got back home, through the night. The horses whinnied and kept on treading on as Danniger looked ahead for a couple seconds before giving his answer. "I think we'd better rest, getting lost out here is not a good idea, and the wolves are going to be attracted to these bloody bodies we have with us." He said cooly, hoping Schantinger with all his normal stubborn insistence would let it pass. Schantinger also thought a while, swinging back and forth with the walking of the horses. "Well, he said, after awhile, I guess I'll let you have your way you old scudder ruff you." He said it, calmly, almost to lighten the real meaning of his words. The Captain simply smiled and looked straight ahead. He was glad that his companion had enough sense to take his advice.

The sun again sunk deep along the horizon, as they worked their way back through the dark woods, the shades of black, gray, purple, and orange red filled the narrow paths they took and danced along the ground as they found a decent place to sleep, or attempt to do so. They made some strong coffee, and would get little sleep chasing the wolves and coyotes away form their thousand pounds of meat and three hundred pounds of skins. Schantinger would no doubt complain all night long, but it was a good load of virtually free meat they would get, and they, or at least The Captain considered it worthwhile. They were back home by ten the next morning.

Nearly Spring

The Captain had been enjoying the dark, almost black, low fat roasts of his bison. This was an increasingly rare thing, to be able to take bison in the wild. In another few years they would be all but extinct. It was good though that he could still take a little piece of the West for free. As the Winter droned on, he had come to think and ponder a bit after suppers at the house. He was reflecting on how things had changed in town, the valley, and in fact The West. It was not the place he had come to, it was a different place, one that in some ways he did not recognise. They were his autumn years that he had entered into, if he admitted it or not. It was his time in life to reflect, to think, and to finally perhaps make some sense of life. He had always been a man

with a direction to go, something to conquest, and something to do. Now it seemed he was running out of reasons to do things. He said to Rebecca one night, his old briar in his hand,
just grabbing it for an after supper smoke, "What do you think about becoming a State?" She looked at him not knowing exactly what he meant, and then it dawned on him, he meant the Territory becoming a State, not her herself becoming one. She said "I'm not sure Captain, it will mean more schools, and roads, and laws. That's for sure. But what else, I'm not sure. It would be nice to have a little more civility around here, I'd say. It's not a bad thing to become part of the Union. I can't imagine anything much wrong with it." She stopped a bit, looking at the food before them, noticing it was becoming cold. "Why do you ask me this all of a sudden?" She asked now. He looked around the room, his eyes glancing around a little and said, after awhile "I just think it's IMPORTANT, don't you? I mean, it changes our lives afer all, doesn't it?" She just remembered his southern drawl, it having both faded as he moved further north, and it becoming just part of him, that is his personality, that she had come to take for granted, as if he was a part of her, and would never change. He continued " Yes, it means that we'll have more taxes, more issues, and more to worry about, don't you think?" Rebecca knew it was

an argument that would end no-where, and just
decided to let it pass, saying "Well honey, I know it
does, but we can't do much about it, now can we?"
That was the end of the conversation, for then and
they went on to clean up and set the dishes away. He
was sure to think and talk about it again though. It
would not be too long either. It was inevitable that
his life would change, and just then he came to
realize it. The world around him was changing, and
while he had not noticed it, he too had changed.
Things being as they were, they would continue to
do so. While he might think things were stationary,
they are not, nothing in the world is the same
forever. His
eye's blink in the whole universe of time, in reality
was nothing. He had been doing this, and doing that
for decades, each one seemingly real to him,
seemingly important and to some extent everlasting,
but none of it was.

The Captain and Jenny were out on one of their
rides, and they could feel Spring in the April air.
Spring would seem to come late in Montana. The
Captain remembered how early Spring would come
in Georgia at his boyhood home. It would be very
warm even in March. He took the old Bay and the
Pinto out to get them in shape for the work they'd
be doing soon. The grass had started to green, and

the horses clip-clopped their way through the Winter-beaten ground. It was flat, and still quite muddy, as the horses made their way across some of the lower pastures. It was chilly when the wind blew even though overall it was warming. The sky was the bluest blue of any blue you could imagine, with wisps of thin white clouds making their appearances every once in a while. The Captain looked up into the sky, he had cleaned his square crowed tan hat, and it rode high on his head, making him look taller. His daughter noticed the slight peculiarity of him wearing his hat high and looking into the sky. "What are you thinking about?" She asked. "What's so interesting?" He smiled at her and said "Oh nothing much." In fact he was very much bothered by the changes that had occurred over the past few years they were there, but he didn't want her to know it. She continued " So what are we going to be doing the next season? Are the hands going to be coming back from Texas, or wherever they are?" The truth was he did not really know himself. Rebecca had been bothering him about them, every year he had to get some new ones, or bring the old ones back. It was unreliable, but now business was slowing down. There were so many ranchers now, and so many people, no longer did people need cattlemen to run the doggies the long distances they had before, or to round up stock or wild heads of cattle and bring

103

them in. While he didn't realize it, he was tired; tired in a way that creeps up on a man, and catches him off guard. "I'm sure some will show up sooner or later." He finally said. "Why do you ask?" He said looking at her. She said in reply "Because mother's been talking about it, how you should just forget about it and retire. "What! Really!" He exclaimed. Why is that?" She drew her face down now in somewhat of a frown, saying "Well, you can't work FOREVER, now can you? Is all she meant, after all, you're a rich man aren't you daddy? Why would you want to have MORE when you already have so much?" He couldn't believe the level of maturity his daughter showed, nor even the fact it was obvious she was a grown woman.

He was considering his next venture, he thought it might be high time to buy more land before the Swedes and everybody else bought it all up. Was he ready for that though he thought? He felt like he was prepared to keep on raising cattle. His desire to be more and do more was still in him, burning like a lighthouse light, driving him on to the next horizon and the next, never being satisfied with what he had. He though he was ready to keep on, but he wasn't. He knew on a subconscious level that the end of this life was over, but his conscious mind was not quite ready for it. He wanted to grab what of the Old

West he could before it was too late. But it already was too late. He wasn't ready to continue though, maybe it was high time he ended his career. But his ambition drove him on, made him blind to the fact the West was no longer the West, and his budding daughter had enough sense to know it.

The Spring

While it was a pleasant life they had, it was not perfect, life went on like this for the rest of the Winter, and into Spring. The Captain grew more restless as he pondered deeper and deeper into the fact that Schantinger was no longer the young vibrant businessman he used to be but an old stick in the mud. He inquired about any free land adjacent to the ranch, and Schantinger told him it was all taken up. As it came time to hire more hands, and get some stock, he wanted to do it, but there was less reason to do so. So many people were doing the same. His daughter was fully grown, and The West itself had grown. It was no longer the wild place he had know. Now he did not know what to do. The Mestizos, all except Juan spread to warmer climes, during winter. He was curious if any would arrive on his door step this Spring. The Captain had little things to do, this and that The Captain and Rebecca were fairly close, but Jenny remained fairly distant, of course it may very well be the way with teenage girls, yet it was time for her to get out of the house and start a life of her own. He was by no means a sensitive man, but he was curious if he and his wife were as close as they should be. He was so curious about it in fact that he asked his dear friend Larry Clayton about it.

Danniger walked into the old rotting farm house on the other side of town. It was dark inside and he could not make head or tails of where he was. "Where are you? You old fool Larry Clayton!" He finally yelled, frustrated with the game his friend was playing on him. "For heaven's sake man, why don't you turn on some lights?" Regardless of it being the middle of the day, Clayton had the house shut up like a mausoleum, and there was a grayish darkness to the room. Finally, after standing just past the living room table, an old oaken affair, beaten and used, Danniger's friend finally emerged, grinning out of the darkness. "For heaven's sake, can't you see in the dark man?" Larry said, chuckling a little as he did. He was a big man, taller than Danniger, about six feet two inches. He had a dirty tannish hat on, stained with sweat. "Ha ha ha, ha, ha." Clayton laughed at his joke. It was a stupid thing really, he expected Danniger to come by and then leave all the windows closed so nothing could hardly be seen when Danniger came in out of the light. "Oh!" He said, still laughing. " I'm sorry, you old fool. I really am. Now what can I do for you?" Clayton could hardly keep his composure, and was now trying to straighten up from being doubled over with laughter.

The two men sat down and by and by had a little whiskey. Danniger looked out over the fields that led back into town, listening to Larry's discourse on his family, and how they were doing. They were doing well. His two sons were grown men, finding jobs in the cities, and his daughter had married a local merchant. Life was pleasant. "So what brings you over here?" Clayton finally asked his old friend as he leaned back in the old oak chair pushing his hat back to expose his eyes. "There must be some reason you wanted to sneak into a dark house." Danniger ignored his friend's little joke. Danniger finally got the courage to ask and said "Well, you know things are changing around here quite a bit. It's not the wild place it used to be." He trailed off, and it seemed his friend certainly could agree with that. Larry's long black beard shook up and down a bit as he nodded in agreement. Larry said "Yeah, I agree with that, there's
no doubting that. The fact is that we can't do anything about it, so why fret" There was a slight pause again, as the two men thought a little,

contemplating, though they were not the type of men who normally contemplate anything. Larry again spoke "Yeah, the fact of the matter is, we don't have control of things, we like to think we do, but in reality, we are just part of the Country, this Nation that is. We can't hardly say what happens or what don't. We can only control our own selves and hope that it works out for the best." Danniger agreed, though he had not really thought about it before. Danniger spoke this time "You know to be honest that isn't why I came over today. And not to get tripped in the dark either. The reason why, is I'm just curious did you and Susan always get along just perfect? I'm thinking these past few weeks, that I don't really even understand Rebecca, and beside that, I think now that over all these years we never really even understood each other." Larry looked at him and said "Well! That's a sort of big surprise when you think about it, isn't it?" He looked at his friend a couple seconds and then continued "You know Captain, I've been what, married as long as you? Maybe longer, maybe shorter, but the thing I've noticed is that men and women just plain think different, there's no way a man is really ever going to understand how a woman thinks, that's the end of it. I can't hardly imagine that a man would ever have a chance at understanding them." There was another brief pause. While Danniger understood what his friend was saying, and in fact his own experience proved it so, it was fairly shocking to hear it coming out of his mouth. In time Danniger responded, speaking slowly at first and then speeding up his pace "Yes, yes that's right isn't it. You know I never really thought about it, but you're right. That's the truth of it, isn't it?" They paused again each thinking it over. Danniger said again "That's a lucky thing to know I guess, as long as you're prepared to think it." Larry just chuckled, because they both knew it was true. Danniger started again "So where does that leave us then? What are we supposed to do then?" His friend responded "Honestly Captain, I don't think there's a whole lot we can do. It's the way of the world you know." While his friend's answer made sense, it was not what he expected. He expected maybe it would all make sense, and his friend could tell him that it was just a phase or something, but he didn't. He confirmed that he like all men, have some problem understanding what it is that make women work. While his own experience had proven to him it was true, hearing it come out of someone else's mouth was a huge shock. It was just with this past season that he started to think about all these things. He was surprised that Larry saw things more or less the same way he did. He was also, now, after thinking about it, surprised that he had not thought about it earlier. The misunderstandings about how to deal with the wild horses, the expectations of this or that, and how to raise their daughter, they all lead to the same conclusion: that they just didn't understand each other, and maybe never did. Even through he enjoyed the courting in Georgia and their early years in Texas, now it seemed as if it was just a juvenile game. He was in love with the idea of love, and not with the reality of life with that woman.

Danniger went into town to visit Schantinger again at his office. He wanted to check up with him and see if there weren't any plots of land available. "No, ... no I'm afraid there are no more near you Captain." Schantinger looked up from his desk now and to Danniger and outside to the windows and street. It was at last getting green outside. "No, all the damn West has been bought up, at least round these parts." The Captain's disappointment was palpable. He went back home, after a quick drink at The Old Horseshoe tavern.

Rebecca was waiting for him, she was always waiting for him. She had waited for him for almost twenty years now. She would stand by him, regardless of what happened because that is who she was. Though it would seem the scales had dropped from his eyes, he still loved her, and would try his

110

best to make sense of things. He didn't know if he would understand her, though he wanted to. Larry had almost convinced him it was a preordained thing that men and women will not understand each other. He had lived with her twenty years though, he would like to think he understood her. The old horse trotted through the gate that lead to the ranch, he could see Rebecca sitting on the porch after a long and hard Winter. It was nice to see her there again. The fresh tips of new grass were everywhere, springing up and saying hello to the world again. The gate was long, and stretched across the road wide enough to allow two wagons to pass each other. The gate was made of long thin poles tied together. She stood up and smiled as he came in, happy to see him.

The West was not the West that they had come to, nor were they the people that had come west. Rather, they were old hats at things. They were the type of people that were able to do things, and did not make much of whatever came their way. Now, The Captain had come to realize that things are not solid, that Rebecca could be what he thought she was, or could very well be someone entirely different. The kind and direct advise of his old and tough friend Larry rang true in his ears. He realized that as he aged things did not look he same. Maybe

111

they were not the same, maybe he was not the same, and maybe it was that for the first time he was seeing things as they really are. The past few months it seemed as if she and he just didn't see things the same as far as how the ranch and everything should run. She wanted him to retire, but he wasn't ready to. As he thought about it, it seemed that maybe all the small little arguments they had in the past were maybe the same; they just didn't understand each other.

He smiled back at Rebecca, saying hello, and asking if she had seen any cowboys come in from anywhere. She had not. She had waited a long time for this day to come, her woman's intuition told her that he had the talk with Schantinger that was going to come sooner or later. It was time that The Captain put by the things of the past, and live in the now. It was time that the wild, uncouth, rough place she both loved, and sometimes hatted come to a sort of end. The Captain's high days were over, and finally she could simply enjoy life with him.

The Second Noble Truth
Suffering is Caused by Wanting

North Georgia 1862

"God damn those Yankees!" William Danniger said, as he shot his Springfield rifled musket and slid back behind the embankment. Boom! Boom! The Union cannon roared as they tried to get access to the river the South was trying to hold. The cannon balls would make huge thuds and mud would fly everywhere as they crashed into the ramparts the South had made at the edge of the small river, which was about one hundred yards across. Whoosh, boom! Another ball crashed over Danniger's head. "God almighty that was a close one? Wasn't it Corporal?" He yelled, his voice raising pitch toward the end of the sentence. "I think it's high time we try to get our ass out of here, or return some fire, isn't it?" The Corporal wasn't sure what to do. It seemed as if their chances of getting out alive were becoming slimmer and slimmer as each man on their side fell. The cannon men, on the opposite side of the river were doing what they could though.

Another ball thudded into the embankments. It was

a cross between a smack and a whop that it made. The Corporal said, in his Virginian accent "It seems, private, that we may have to take evasive action, and get ourselves out of here." By this Danniger did not understand exactly what the man said. If he was saying they definitely should retreat, or if it seemed as if they may have to do so. Whoosh, boom! Another Yankee cannon ball hit, about twenty yards from their position. "Damn!" Danniger yelled again. Then the Southern troops answered back with two cannons. Whoo, whoo, they made a sort of whizzing noise as the shots flew through the air. Splat, crack! Their balls went, hitting God knows what on the Yankee side.

It was a long, and drawn out affair; Danniger and that group of thirty odd Southerners holding that position while the North tried to shoot them out of their reenforcements, till one side won. The South did hold the river position though and Danniger was able to claim some valuable experience. He, along with his comrades had done a good day's work. They could all be proud, and Danniger, as a young military man could say it was a day he moved forward in his career. He was not a warrior at heart. He was still a young man, and yearning to find himself in the world. He did believe in the Southern cause though. He though it just that they should be able to live as they so choose, and keep their traditions. Still, he was not a born fighter, he was more of a thinker and a problem solver. He didn't see much reason to go around shooting at people without good cause, but taking a man's property and way of life certainly was a good enough cause for him.

The Captain, in short order became a Sargent. He had enlisted in the Rebel Army to fight The War Between the States for the Southern States' rights to their way of life and traditions. He had started as a thirty-three-year-old new recruit and had promise to make something of himself in the Army. He was a passionate Southern who believed in the cause, and had good wits about him. He could lead men, and would prove himself time and time again on the battlefield.

These were the days he was courting Rebecca. They meet at a mutual friend's house. He would come to visit his friend's fine house and it just so happened that the woman he was to marry happened to be there on one occasion. He was a budding Army man, and she a resident of Athens Georgia. She was not a wealthy woman, but she came from a good family. It was in Georgia that he would first find out what he was capable of doing, and would strike out in that pursuit of doing as much as he could as fast as he could. It was in those early skirmishes that he learned early on he was a man able to do things. As he worked up in rank he would have the opportunity to charge back in forth in front of the troops, his big white horse snorting and prancing as he encouraged the men to do the impossible and reminded them of the importance of the moment. They were in historic times, and their traditions, and right to live as they wished were in jeopardy. He, even as a young man realized the unique and special place in history they found themselves. It helped rally the men and make them want to follow Danniger. They realized, through his interpretation of the circumstances how important the seconds and minutes they were about to live were. How critical every action in every second of battle is critical to how the future would unfold and how history would remember them. Danniger fought till the bitter end of the War. What he saw, like many was horrific, and he would not forget it. He was a strong, and unsentimental man though, at least at the time, and he did not let the stench or war, or the horrors it brought down upon society phase him. William "Tecumseh" Sherman said that people think war is all glory, but it is in fact hell. The Captain to be certainly learnt this first had during the War, but he was not too affected by it.

He used the War to become better. A better leader, and a wiser citizen. He came to realize the difficulty in life, and that life is not perfect.

Danniger started the War a young man, not knowing the extent to which man could hate and destroy his brethren all to hell. He did not know the extent to which all life can be pulled away from a man in one night of terror, how abysmal one man can act against his neighbour when intoxicated by his own sense of right and wrong. He started the War as a young energetic man wishing to protect his homeland, and by the end, his philosophy of life was developed. He saw the struggles of the War as the struggles of life, and how circumstances pitted man against man, and man against his own self. He saw the horribleness of it all and grew up during the War, he became a citizen of the real world for the first time; not a citizen of his ambitions and dreams, but a citizen of the real world, of real people and real struggles.

Virginia 1862

"Sargent! Sargent! The Yankees are coming! The Yankees are coming!" The future Captain's horse reared back, not liking the wild running of the young private as the young man charged back behind the lines and through the blockades. It was not normal practice to allow a Sargent to be in charge of a band of soldiers, but desperate times called for desperate measures. It was just past ten at night and had been dark about two hours. The Yankees had waited till dark to move and try to sneak past the troops they knew were somewhere in the woods blocking the way to the Fort.

The opposing sides were much closer to each other than one might imagine, and the murky blackness of the night distorted their views. It wasn't long before one side saw the other. The Yankees saw the shine of one of the Southern soldier's musket barrels, and quickly spread the word. It was not long before The Yankees put up a position and started blasting with cannon and mortar in the direction they thought the Southerners were. They wanted to blast a path to the Fort as they went rather than try to find the exact position of the troops. The possibility of capture made a rough approach better than one of fine tactics. It was a messy business. Cannon balls crashed through the trees, and the Rebels made a charge where they could see the Yanks, charging, yelling, and stabbing anything that moved.

It was The Sargent's first opportunity to lead men in battle, and they were less than ideal circumstances.

The area they had to cover was so widespread that it was impossible to have an officer in command of each and every band of soldiers. So it was his bad luck to have the Yankees try to barge through his area. He tried to rally his men around and spread word, but without a clear idea of where the Yankees were, or how many, it was difficult to start an offensive. He spread the word as quickly and quietly as possible. The Yanks had already started shooting so it was futile to try to form any positions to attack. He sent runners out to try to find the troops so they could try to attack from the flanks. All the while the cannon balls were crashing through the trees. Then the screaming began. The young boys of the troop were getting hit, maybe it would seem just in their minds, and start simply going crazy, running from the lines, hollering, and yelling to God, their mothers, anybody. "God Damn it, where the hell are those damn Yankees?!" The Sargent said, peering out into the dark Virginia woods. "If there's anything I hate, it's a Yankee." The privates came in reporting to him, and it would seem the Yankees also had runners in the woods, trying to find them. It would seem they found out how far spread the Rebels were and decided to start to blast their way through. It seemed a messy sort of business, but under the circumstances maybe it was the best they could do.

"How many are there? How MANY ARE THERE?!" The Sargent yelled, trying to get an idea of what he was up against. His scream was wild, and out of control. It was the yell of a newborn child not knowing where or who he is. It was a desperate scream in the dark of confusion, wishing to have some idea of where and what might be. It would seem there were a few hundred, many more than his tiny band could handle. He regained his composure, relaxing his face, saying, now softer "Get the couriers and tell them to send word to Cornel Hastings and Galliger. Let them know there is a column of them coming in and we need reenforcements." They were off into the woods, their horses running as if Satan himself were after them. Their horses' hooves beat the ground like mallets, and the animals' nostrils flared out like trumpet bells, as they tore over thicket, woods, and fields. The men got word to the others, about three miles away in either direction and rallied themselves to help The Sargent. Meanwhile, The Sargent was positioning the troops as high as he could. They got a fairly good idea of where the Yankees were, positioned their cannon and let fly. It was a terrible business, the red flares of the cannon, the screaming of the young boys, and the uncertainty of it all contributed to a nasty and bloody business. Finally it would seem they found the outlines of the North's lines, and could start their true offensive. They saw how the Union positioned their cannon. The Union troops were inside the lines of cannons. The troops were waiting for the cannon to open ground before slowly moving forward. The Sargent tried his best to take out the Union cannon before sending anyone out. It would be an outright slaughter if he let the mass of hundreds of Yankees lose on his tiny bands. As the Sargent got an idea of where the Union's troops were he positioned himself the best he could to oversee the battle and command his men. The sharpshooters and cannon blasted away at the Yankees where they could, picking them out of the darkness. Now they had turned the tables on the Yankees, and they had sent horsemen all around the country side, running to and fro. The horsemen found out the extent of the Union's troops, and they were vast, a huge swath of them covered the country, what they could make out was a mass of dark purple-hued shapes, like lumps all over the countryside, but there was an eventual end to them. As fast as they could Galliger and Hastings sent brigades to the south and north of the Union troops, and they started cracking down on them. Luckily for the young Sargent, Hastings and Galliger were near enough by to support him, without them he surely would have lost his small band of brothers.

The shooting did not last too long, it would be dawn soon. As the Union saw the Rebs clearly and an idea of where they were they started to retreat, squeezing as quickly as they could out of the pincer hold the South had formed around them. They blasted as they could in retreat, the cracking of tree limbs, earth thudding, and all else horrible noise was behind them, as they panicked, trying to keep the South back. It was clear they would not be able to push on that night and into day. They would have to regroup and take on the South for his piece of land another day.

The Sargent's men thanked him for saving their skins, and rejoiced in the victory. They danced and sung their songs of the South. It was a clear picture that the young Sargent Will Danniger had proven himself in battle. He was an example of success in a comparatively young leader. That was only the beginning though. In someways he was simply lucky, lucky to have support. He was a man interested in rank, and interested in getting as much out of the War as possible. While he started out as a loyal Southerner who believed in the cause, it became obvious that a man could make something of the War. It was obvious that through hard work, and decisive action a man could rise through the ranks and distinguish himself. While he started the War as a person wishing to lend a hand, the desire to gain more and more rank grew in him like a fire. He saw the opportunity to become famous, and rich through Yankee plunder.

The Southern troops congratulated each other on a job well done. The Sargent remarked to some of his compatriots the viciousness of the Yankee attack. Everyone agreed, it was a rough business, but was struck the young Sargent at the time was the pure hellish insanity of it. He found the whole idea that one group of people would start moving out in the middle of the night and start shooting out into the woods to scare out the enemy was as preposterous as the idea of starting a war on Christmas Eve. At first he assumed that the War on both sides would follow some logic, that each with their own ideas of how things should be would systematically fight in such a way as to prove themselves the better of the two, and one side would come out winner. Now it seemed it was just a crazy thrashing through the woods destroying as they went. After the rejoicing was over the band of brothers started talking a little. After-all, it was nearly light out, they had fought all night. They began to reflect on it all. "Sargent." A young private said. "Now that the fighting is over, I would very much like to simply go home." The

123

Sargent realized the point he was making. He was a beaten poor thing that looked more like an old tired dog than a young man. He allowed the young man a release from the Army, even though he needed every man he had.

After the battle Danniger went back to Georgia to visit his beloved, she was doing well and prayed for him every day. While he would not admit it, the War had a hold of him. He was tired after this near-death experience. It had shaken him, but at the same time he enjoyed the rush of the violence and danger. He took a well-deserved rest. His experience in battle had in some ways disillusioned him with the human race, but at the same time instilled in him a desire to do more and change what he could. He knew, even then that chances were slim that the South would win. However the hardness of war built in him a desire to win himself as it were. While the South may lose, he could win, he could get something out of the War. He wanted to gain glory, prestige, and position, and that is exactly what he did. By War's end he went from Private to Captain. He first was a rifleman, one of hundreds in any given battle, but in time proved himself capable of planning attacks and leading men. The negative Karma built in him like a poison. He would lose his youth and innocence in the War. He would be a richer, wiser man, but the

War meant the demise of his soul.

Rebecca came to him that night on the balcony of her parents' home. The Yankees had not destroyed Athens and her parents lived in relative peace. He was standing, smoking a cigar, and taking in the cool Autumn air. They both had come to enjoy the visits they had together during those rushed, unpleasant War years. The night was fresh, with an earthy smell of dirt and moss. The crickets and frogs were still chirping their songs of territory and love. "Well darling?" She cooed at him. Stepping from the room onto the balcony as she spoke, stopping just as she got onto it. "When is the awful War going to be over? It seems it has been forever since I had you home." He knew full well what she meant. She tried to keep a level head about it all, but it was difficult. He could sense her frustration and lack of energy. It was a great energy sapper, and had everyone worried about what the future would bring. She stopped looking at him and walked all the way out onto the balcony now and walked over to the railing herself, looking out and listening to the frogs, sighing, and breathing softly. She did not like the War. It took him away from her and tore everyone's life apart. The Sargent took his attention away from the woods now saying "It will all be over soon enough. I'm doing my best to make what I can of it."

Missouri 1863

The Sargent Will Danniger was now promoted to
Captain. It was not long after his work in Virginia
that the Rebel Army saw him as fit for the title. He
had been sent out to the wild and unpredictable edge
of the war zones. Missouri was a place where chaos
and uncertainty reigned for both North and South.
The Captain was responsible for a medium sized
brigade. He had a long battle record under his belt
now and was well prepared for the wind and
unpredictable theatre that he found himself in. The
South now trusted him fully to be able to make
decisions and that is what he would do. They were
woodsy, muddy, hilly confines that he and his
brigade found themselves in.

"Well Captain." The Captain's first lieutenant said.
"Where do you think we'll find those Yankees?"
They were out on an informational excursion, trying
to see where the Northern troops were. They were
out on horseback, making short excursions into
unknown territory. They had a number of Southern
sympathizers in the farmlands that surrounded them,
but life was uncertain at best. Raiders, wild bands of
opportunists, and general chaos still left everyone in
Missouri at high risk. Captain Danniger was satisfied

with the supporters and informants he had under his wings though, and so far the North had not caught them off guard, so the probability of them falling victim to an informant was low. The Captain was astride a big black horse and was wearing a long gray duster-type coat, it was Autumn, and the seasonal rains had a mist covering the entire area. His companion was dressed similarly. They were overlooking some abandoned pastures that rolled on and on through the countryside. They tried to keep the horses quite, and hide under the trees as much as possible. The fields were damp, and had a soggy layer of mown hay on top of them. Foxes and doves had taken residence among the grass litter, but The Captain had the suspicion beyond them somewhere the Yankees were hiding, and waiting. They were not simple, peaceful fields set aside for a Winter's sleep.

While the War certainly was hell on earth, it offered opportunities to gain rank and prestige. The Captain had the opportunity to lead many men into battle, and he enjoyed it. He lived on through those years like they were the last of his life, for after all, death could well come at any second. He did his duty, and made the best of his life there, among the dead, dying, and wreckage of his homeland. At every opportunity he was promoted, and did not stop putting forth a ceaseless effort until the War was over. The power and authority the loved President Davis bestowed on him was like an elixir to him, and he enjoyed very much the opportunity to both become a noted man, and a leader of a cause he believed in. He learned the subtleties of the human mind, and the strength of the human spirit. He struggled against what he was as an imposing intruder, and also against the rigours of war and life themselves. He learned how to work with people, and how to balance his own mind to live in the horrors of war.

Camps during the War both North and South were interesting places. Card games, music, and boredom were the rule. They brought their guitars, jaw harps, fiddles, and the like and played to pass the time away. For hours, days, or weeks they might camp, cleaning rifles, and passing the time before the horror of war crashed down on them again. The Captain became somewhat philosophical after he entered Missouri. At the end of the War he would still be in one piece though, he would be a man capable of taking on almost anything, or so he thought. By the War's end he would be a much wiser and knowledgeable man, in all the ways of mankind. The War would instill in him a great desire to go out and do something, to grab his destiny, and get the most out of life he could. His ambition would grow with every battle he won, and every rank he achieved. While in some ways he had gone mad, insane with greed for power, he started to understand the nature of life. The desire to gain rank and prestige burned in, and eventually, by the time he had his Montana ranch, would be his undoing.

"It's a message for you Captain." The courier said. The Captain was standing among a few men as the young man approached. His horse trotted proudly through the mess of camp. It was a tall tan horse, nearly too tall for the tiny young private. The young man got off the horse and gave the bound-up papers to The Captain. It was a letter of congratulations on his good work in Virginia. He thanked the young man heartily and took it into his tent to read. They would be two more days in that particular camp, then, The Captain's horse spies found a small band of Northern sympathisers. The Captain would often send lone horsemen around, usually by dark to assess the surroundings. The Captain rallied his men, surrounded them and shot them all. They didn't know what hit them. Many of the Missouri campaigns were like this, and in fact most the fighting in the War Between the States was in Missouri. It was an unorganized business though, and The Captain didn't care for it one bit. He liked the pomp and circumstance of the great eastern battles. He was satisfied with himself though, and the recognition he got both from President Davis, and from his fellows in the Army built up a satisfaction and desire to do more.

"Shhh, be quiet!" The Captain said, trying to keep his voice down. They were hunkered down in some make-shift earthworks and it became apparent that the Yankees were nearby. They received word from the spies that Yankees were near, and indeed they were. They could seem them, coming and going in twos or small groups in and out of the area to get supplies, relieve themselves in the woods, and the like. "Do you see them Lieutenant?" The Captain asked, keeping his voice down and peering over the earth wall with his brass spyglass. "I can see the tops of their heads. They are about a mile away in those woods. We're lucky they haven't found us. Or maybe they have and are waiting to do something about it." There was a hesitance in his voice, for The Captain liked to be sure of things, and this particular circumstance did not make it easy for him to be sure. "How many do you think there are Sir?" The Lieutenant asked. The Captain looked as far as he could in either direction around the bobbing heads he saw. "Are you sure they're Yankees?" The Lieutenant continued. The Captain continued to look, the smell of mud and vegetation filled the air around their fortifications and filled his nostrils. He could not make a fair assessment yet. After a while, he admitted "It looks like they've covered no more than a quarter-mile square, as far as I can reckon. I'm not sure what they're doing, maybe just scouting." He was not sure what his next move would be.

Things went on like this for a few days. They were quite lucky the Yankees did not find them, and it was curious that The Yankees did not send a party in their direction and discover them. The Captain, in time came to the conclusion that he had seen the extent of them. He wanted to make SOMETHING happen. The monotony of it all was driving him mad. He had enough experience that he felt confident in his assessments and decided to start some action. The cannon and mortars were placed on either end of the Yankees. The men had to move as quickly as possible to avoid detection, and place themselves before the Yankees got wind of what was happening. The Captain placed his sharpshooters at the tops of the embankments, and gave the command to start firing. It looked like they had the North surrounded and were sure to crush them. The mortars hammered from either side, locking the Yankees into the little depression where they were hiding among the bushes and trees. At the same time the North could not charge up the high embankments The Captain had built. It seemed a lost cause for the North, but then, about thirty minutes into the fighting a line of dragoons came charging from across the field behind the embankments of The Captain. They charged in, firing pistols and The Captain had to make hasty moves to keep from having his unprotected back smashed. "Captain! Captain!" The Lieutenant yelled. "It seems we did not think of the possibility the Yankees might have reenforcements hiding somewhere. I hope it's not all lost." The Yankees poured across the field to the back of the earthworks, and through the little patch of woods between the field and the enforcement. The Southern troops slid down, losing the position of the snipers, and tried to lay low and return fire where they could. The mortars, had decimated the North's troops they were attacking, but were useless on the other side of the embankments to protect The Captain's strong hold.

The Captain did his best to rally the troops, and fight off the Yankees. While those Northerners down below in the hollow of the woods were crushed, the groups running across the fields did not let up. The Captain locked his men in the mud fortress while the horses of the North trampled all over them, the

132

dragoons trying to find whom they could, but not willing to forage out into the woods and take on the mortar and cannon. In about one hour it was all over. The Yankee dragoons ran too and fro trying to find a way to get The Captain out of his den, but they could not.

The Captain had made a grave error and his enthusiasm had gotten the better of him. He knew better than to make such an assumption without any reenforcements nearby, but his boredom along with his history of successes made him complacent. No one would speak the unspeakable truth, but they all knew it, The Captain nearly got them killed. It seemed that he had lost his edge. The rest of the War went on. The Captain went back to the East, where he continued fighting but did not gain any more rank. He would visit Rebecca when he could, sitting on her balcony smoking cigars and reminiscing about the campaigns he won. President Davis saw fit to retire The Captain without much ado, and it was the close of a bloody bit of history.

Eastern Missouri 1864
At Camp

"It's been a rough and bloody business." The Captain said, looking at the men gathered around

133

him in Camp. It was a small camp, just over fifty
men remained with him. It was a mossy wooded
area, hidden away, not far from a rocky outcropping
leading down into a dry river bed. Smoke, the
constant companion of the nineteenth century blew
nonchalantly up, and around Camp, whirling and
fading as it went. The tannish tents all around stood
absorbing the colour and smell of the smoke. The
men were equally tired, most stood and walked
around Camp aimlessly, others were cleaning the
best they could. It had been like this a few days now.
He sat on a rickety camp chair. It was a fabric
folding chair, a length of stripped fabric was held in
a frame and leaned to the left as its legs dug down
into the dirt. They all were dirty. Sanitation was
poor, but they got word that they could retire and
disembark. The Frontier skirmishes in Missouri
would last for some time now, and even long after
the War was over, but for this band, President Davis
said they were all through. A courier had just
brought in the mail, if it could be called that. The
South had a rough system of keeping letters moving
between encampments and the like, a much more
primitive affair than the telegraph that kept the
North in good communication till the end. It was not
great joy they felt, or great sadness either. To them,
it was a sort of numb feeling, for they had already
had their great highs and lows during the entire

length of the campaign. It was a rough and dirty business indeed.

After some sitting around The Captain again spoke, "Well gentlemen, " He said in his soft Southern draw. "It seems our work here is done." He sat a while still, leaning back in his rickety chair, looking out at the gathered men, and the deep woods that surrounded them. He stood now, slowly his bones creaky from the cold months in Missouri. "I would like to thank you all for good service. You have done us all proud, you have stood up to the Tyrant, in the face of oppression and you have fought for what you believed in. I, or anyone else, could not ask you for more."

The War had changed him and the entire Country. It had lost its innocence, and was now in the grasp of hard years in reconstruction. The nature of everything is to change, The Captain was like anyone else, he too would change as his circumstances did. He started as a young boy and now was a hardened man.

Athens Georgia 1865

"Well Becky, the damn War is over, and look at where it's got us!" Danniger told his wife of almost three years. He drowned on, speaking slowly, as he reflected on what he had experienced the past few years, his Southern accent making him draw out his vowels slightly. "We worked like dogs, saw some of the damnedest things a man could imagine, and now where are we." The last three words almost inaudible, as his energy drained from him, the words seeming to take his last breath. He lifted his arm, with some effort to slip the clay pipe he was holding onto the beaten old pine table top. The only bits of furniture they had after the Yankees had run through the town burning and stealing as they went. The house was hot, steamingly hot, and had no glass panes in the windows. The beating Georgia Summer was all around outside and the grasshoppers were chirping their songs. She came around to the back of his chair and comforted him a while, wishing him to forget the past, and live for the future. "It's all over now, but we still have our lives and our freedom honey." She said. "It could always be worse. At least we can start over."

The Captain at that time was not a rich man, the Rebel Army would have a difficult time paying the commissions it promised its officers now. So he was forced to make life for himself. Through hard work and suffering he would have to make the most of it, and do what he could to survive. However, survival alone was not enough for The Captain. He wanted more, he wanted to own something, make something, and mostly create destiny all his own. A destiny he could claim as his own self-created one. "Well, what do you think we should do now Becky?" He asked, picking up his voice a little. "What in all this earth can we do now?" It wasn't a question exactly, but a way of voicing what he was thinking. The blistering heat waved in the windows, and the sun beat down on the roof of the poor old house. She answered, by and by. " We can just start over, that's what we can do. And why not? What's to stop us? We're young, aren't we, we have the backbones to start a new life?" He agreed, for after all there was really no choice in the matter. It would be a difficult matter if people didn't have the ability to start over if the circumstances called for it.

They packed up later that week, taking the two-year-old Jenny with them, made arrangements for Rebecca's family to take over the little house and the rough patch of land. They gathered what they could, which wasn't much, and made out for Texas. It would be a hard few weeks to get there, but word was that many cattle were there for the taking. It would seem the many years of war had allowed many cattle to go feral and roam free wherever they could. Anyone who had the guts to round up the long-horned beasts could take them up to Chicago and the like to sell. After a career as a Captain of the Army, Danniger decided beef could be his new life. They did not know exactly what to expect. They had not much cash to spare, and what they did was in the South's own make. They would have to find what little place they could to live, perhaps squatting somewhere, till they could get back on their feet. It was a risky business, but the life of the Old South was over. There was no hope in getting that back.

"Alright pa, alright ma, don't worry, I can take care of things." The Captain lifted his eyes briefly up from what he was doing to look at his in-laws. They could see the obvious lack of energy he had, but he was trying his best to pick up his spirits. He loaded the last few things into the old rickety wagon and said his good byes to his in-laws, wondering when he might see them again. They didn't know if they really believed that everything would be taken care of, but under the circumstances didn't have much choice. They trusted their son-in-law with their daughter's life, so it was most likely not risky, or at least too risky. They waived their goodbyes, the heat beating down on them and the wagon started its creaky journey to parts unknown. They had a pair of mules and a horse that the Yankees hadn't slaughtered. It was rough going. They would have to follow what roads they could, and hope not to be taken by some road gang. Road gangs, violence, and uncertainty followed Reconstruction of the South for many years. They would partly have to make roads as they went, following what they could, cutting what they couldn't. It would be rough on the baby, but it was the best they could do. Along the journey they saw the remains of Cherokee and Shawnee villages, destroyed plantations, roving bands of Rebels who didn't think the War was over, Union troops doing reconnaissance, and unbearable heat. In time though they made it into Texas, and sure enough the wild herds of longhorns were there, there for the picking.

Texas 1865

"Well Rebecca, what do you think? At least we're alive" The Captain said, sitting down after a long day rounding up some cowboys. They had arrived in Texas about one week ago and found a nice little place near a small creek. The lad was said to be no body's and was up to whomever would squat on it, at least for now. They had built a lean-to type of structure, and were planning on a corral and barn. It was somewhat scrubby land, a few pines dotted the landscape, it was mostly dry, and not much good for farming, but the wild herds of longhorns came and went as they pleased. It was part of the land annexed from Mexico some years before, and had a wild spirit to it that was hard to define.

He sat down in a make-shift chair made of some odd pieces of tree they found and an old blanket. He was covered with dust from head to toe, and sweat dripped from his broad-brimmed hat. He exhaled loudly, and looked out at the expanses of dust and scrubby trees that surrounded them. "How's the baby?" He asked looking at Rebecca to his side and lifting his sweat-stained hat up to get a better look. She sat a moment or two, looking at him and replied "Fine, just fine, we're doing fairly well for ourselves thank you." She smiled her sheepish smile, meaning what a silly question it was. "Yes William, we are doing well considering the circumstances." She continued. "We are settling in fairly well, considering we're living practically outside like the Indians." He cast his eyes back onto the wild expanses that surrounded them, saying "Oh Rebecca you shouldn't think badly of the Indians, why should we look down at them?"
There was no response from his wife. She just wanted to have some level of comfort after all the War years and the un-godly month-long overland journey they just made, she was ready for a break.

Of course a break would be long in coming because it would be some months before a proper house could be built.

Texas 1866
At the New Homestead

Rebecca and the Captain had a new born child, and now after some months of hard work a Corral, cabin, and a barn was built. Jenny was a pleasant child, but the hot weather of the plains had her cranky at times. The Captain was running out of wild longhorns to gather up as time went on. He had run up into the Midwest on several occasions, taking the long difficult path many times. The era of the long drive would be over soon, and there would be cattlemen all over, just a short distance from Chicago and Kansas City. The railroad brought people, and the option of loading cattle all the way from San Francisco to Chicago on it.

They had built a good life, Danniger and his wife. She was wondering if another child would come into their lives, but it did not seem that it would be. The Ranch was doing well though. The few hands they hired from time to time were enough and they were fairly well satisfied. Still, she, as well as he knew that

141

it would not last forever. Just as the long horns were not going to last, The Ranch would not either. The heat and desolation of the place was too much to live in forever.

Colorado 1868

The Captain was working as a translator and scout. The West had been kind to him. As Rebecca had the ranch in Texas all working smoothly he naturally decided to strike out and find new territory to explore. It was a beautiful and wonderful experience he had so far. The high, purple mountains were such a contrast to the low, hot plains of Texas, it was a breath of fresh air literally. He had the opportunity to mix with many of the local tribes, and learned their languages. He worked for travellers, merchants, and the Government. He was leading parties across the mountains, into the adjoining territories, and also worked as an interpreter for those who needed his services.

The Captain was a man of many talents, and naturally he felt that he should strike out and make the most of what the Country had to offer. He had lost some of his youthful ambition since the War years. He had lost that wild desire to squeeze every last thing out of what surrounded him. Now, he was more willing to take what came his way, but at the same time he was not going to sit around and wait for opportunity to come to him. He still had a fire in his belly and a desire to grab what he could while he could. It was a long journey he had made to get into the mountains, and he felt he may as well make the most of it.

He stayed where he could in Colorado. Good housing was not easy to find. Shacks, lean-toes, shelters of all types he would use as he travelled from settlement to settlement, all-the-while making what he could of life. He made many contacts while he was living there, mostly among the Federal Officials that came tramping through for his reason or that, but also among would-be treasure seekers, ranchers, and the like. It was an interesting life, but after a short time he decided that there was little to keep him in the area.

Northern Plains 1870
In the Cold Winter

The Captain had struck out to see what the Plains had to offer. He was keen to sell the ranch in Texas for as much as possible and start anew in Montana Territory. They were quite wealthy now, their Texas holdings doing well for them. The itch to see and do

143

more was in him though and so he struck out to see what he could manage. He was seeing a wild part of the Country, or at least the Territories that he had not seen before, and was taken aback by the vastness and emptiness of it all. He had fallen in a sort of love with a Sioux woman. She was tall and thin, and her long straight hair whipped in the winds that hammered down out of the distant mountains. She smiled, and her eyes seemed to gleam and smile in their own way. To him, she was mysterious, interesting, and had a noble roughness to her. It was the same noble spirit that embodied the land all around them.

The Captain was still a scout. He was working with the Army to settle some disputes over treaties with the Indians and the settlers. He had come to know Weeping Wolf through his many transmigrations of the territory. She was a widow 30 years of age, her husband died on a buffalo hunt. She welcomed him into her life in all its transitory beauty. It would not be long before she, as well as her way of life were gone forever.

"Sir?" Weeping Wolf said in a soft tone. She was standing out in the open, a wind blew her from side to side. She was wrapped in a buffalo robe. It was thick and wooly. The hair of the robe opened and moved with every gust of wind, and she had to grip her feet into the ground to keep her balance. "Sir, what are you doing?" She asked The Captain. She was wondering what he was planning to do that day. Her English was not very good, so she asked in her own way if he intended to go out, or stay in. He had been staying with her alone, away from her people a short few weeks. She had a little shelter built. He was spending his time mostly travelling and would only occasionally stay with her, though he did visit her often enough to consider her home as a base of operations. He replied to her after a moment or two. He was cleaning up after breakfast. "I am going to go out to visit the Army again today. Don't worry I'll be back soon."

He went on to visit the Army like he had done for so many months before. Things went on like that for some time. It seemed that while life was interesting in Colorado, there would be little chance of him starting a new ranch or such there. It was a wild and rocky place. Though he would in the years to come think from time to time about the months he spent there, regardless of the difficulty there. He would think from time to time of Weeping Wolf and what she was doing.

Texas 1871

"Rebecca? Rebecca, where are you?" The Captain
had returned after his adventures. He stepped inside
the log cabin they had built. It was dry and dusty
outside, and dark inside. He could not make out
much of the interior. He called out because he did
not see her immediately. The many days on the trail
made him tired and disoriented. She was caring for
the child and did not hear him right off. At first she
thought it was someone outside, far away, she did
not know when to expect him. Then as she heard his
footsteps in the front, she knew it was her long-lost
husband. She was in a back room and rushed out to
see him. Rebecca was happy to see him. It was a
hard time for her to stay all alone. Life was pleasant
enough, but it was hard on a woman. Still, she was
able and could handle the hardships of isolation, as
well as the dusty scrabble of the Texas plains. She
wore an old gray dress with little yellow flowers
patterned all over it. It was worn
from hard months of work, and her face was
somewhat dusty itself. They embraced each other.
She smiled in that way that only she could. "I'm glad
you're back you, old 'possum you." She said quietly
in his ear. She squeezed him a little with one arm as
she shifted her weight and looked up at him. He
looked at her not saying a thing for a few seconds.

It would be a few months before The Captain got the idea to actually move to Montana Territory. He had seen thought about it for sometime, after his travels to the Great Plains, and he thought one evening to ask Rebecca about it. It just so turned out that to be one of the most important chapters in his life. From that day forward he had changed his destiny. The whole of what he had experienced and done before was leading to this point, where the next chapter of his life would begin and he would start to turn the circle of existence.

The Third Noble Truth
There is a Place Free from Suffering

Montana Territory 1883

The Captain had spent so much of his life striving for things, and he had forgotten what it was like to simply be. As he reflected on the activities over the past few years, and his talk with Larry Clayton, it seemed he had done enough. He and Rebecca had decided to take it easy and he would take the Mestizos back to Texas to bid them farewell for the last time. He would visit the many friends they had there still, and look at the old Ranch they had sold so many years before.

It had been discussed over a matter of two months, but both of them knew that ultimately the day would come sooner or later when they would retire. The hands knew it themselves, because their lives were transitory ones from the very beginning.

The morning was crisp and fresh as The Captain stepped out of the old house they had built. He pulled his big Stetson down to keep the cool breezes off his neck. The mountains shown bluish-black in the background as the first bright yellow rays of the sun pierced the horizon. He stepped into the dusty yard and looked over in the direction of the workers' quarters. It was difficult for his old eyes to see, especially in the new light. After a few seconds he was able to make out some movement. It looked as if they were putting their blankets out to get the dust out of them. The saddles too were being put out to get a fresh coat of bear grease in preparation for the long journey they had ahead. The Captain had kriss-crossed the country more times that he cared to remember. He had travelled back and forth to see Rebecca during the War, had struck out to find new territory, had faced the mountains as a scout, and now he was taking his men back from where they had come. It was a mixed feeling he felt. It was a happiness and a sadness too. He was not sure what to make of himself, but they seemed to not mind the whole business much, for after-all they knew it was only a matter of time. They stepped out of the living quarters, one at a time looking up at the blinding sun and chattering in their stereotypical way. They smiled and greeted The Captain. He was like a father to them. Together, he and the boys had accomplished a great deal. The particular individuals making up "the boys" had certainly changed from year to year, but still The Captain knew full well that he never could have made anything of the Ranch without them.

"Canso, ... Canso." The Captain said slowly, greeting his friend. They embraced in a brief bear hug as the brown-faced Mexican American walked from behind the fence around the living quarters. The Captain did not allow Canso to stop completely but stopped him in mid-stride. Canso did not mind though and steadied himself by trying to squeeze the guts out of the old man.

"Senor, My friend. How are you today?" Canso asked as he stepped away, getting his bearings. He smiled at his long-time friend. They both knew this day would come. The exact circumstances of course were difficult to predict, but they both knew sooner or later, in some shape or form their parting would come. "So Senor." He now continued, looking up into the face of the old grizzled man. "Now it is our day. Our day, that we knew would come. That we knew would come, someday." They both knew it was true. Not just true, but as true as anything could possibly be.

They got on their horses, Canso, The Captain, Juan, Diego, and all the others and started riding. The poor horses had an idea of the ordeal there were about to endure. They could sense that they would be going farther than they had ever gone before. The expanses of the plains, the rough, rugged lands of west Texas, and more they would see. Long, empty expanses of nothingness would go on forever. The animals did their duty though, not complaining, but simply putting one hoof in front of the other. It would be dry, dirty, dusty, and often dangerous. They would have to stop to rest many times along the journey. The Mestizos knew full well what was in store for them. The animals had a sense of it though, they could sense the importance and finality of the journey that lay ahead.

Northern Great Plains 1883

"Good God in heaven I'm tired!" The Captain exclaimed. He and his men were in a single line riding southeast. They were moving fairly slowly, the horses just swaying back and forth with each step. He was covered from head to toe in mud, dirt, dust, soot, and sweat. They had been travelling for a month now, and he needed a good rest. He knew that his old haunts were nearby. He would take advantage of the trip to see the old places he knew before. He would try to see if Weeping Wolf the Sioux lady he knew more than ten years before might still be around. The towns had grown up considerably all around the Plains. He could hardly believe how much it had changed in such a short amount of time.

They all agreed that a good long rest was in order. They found a spot with a fair amount of tree cover and a slow-moving brook. "Yes, yes!" Canso said, weary from the many days of travel. He could hardly say much more. They straggled over to the water, taking off belts, shirts, and other items as they collapsed on the stream bank, drinking, taking impromptu baths, and the like.

It would not be long before Danniger started his hunt for Weeping Wolf. The others were happy to rest a couple days before continuing and this was just enough time for him to search around and see if he could find her. He searched the towns and Indian villages all around a twenty mile radius, but all to no avail. Finally in Clarke Ville he stepped into a dusty and worn old dry goods store where an old man, who looked to be twice as old as the old derelict shop sat behind the counter. The old man was thin, very thin, almost malnourished looking. He had a thin white beard, scraggly, and dirty looking. Danniger stepped up to the man, the dry pine floor boards creaked as he walked. The old man shifted his weight slightly at Dannigers approach and croaked out a greeting. Danniger made his own courtesies and asked if the old man knew of Weeping Wolf or where she might be. "Gone." The old man said after a long pause. "Gone, passed

away. Died about two?" He picked his voice up at
the end of the sentence, not sure, then went on.
"Two, maybe years ago? Yes. It must of been just
about two I think." Danniger asked "How did you
know her then?" The old man again took his time in
answering. "Oh, I just knew her as somebody who
lived around here." He stopped and looked at
Danniger, saying "Say, what do you want to know
all this for anyhow?" The room became silent for a
second or two while Danniger gathered his thoughts.
He answered the old man in time. "I was a friend of
hers, knew her while I was passing through." The
old man stood up, starting to let his guard down and
answered. "Well sir, I'm sorry to say that she was
killed by the small pox, came through here a few
years back and got to nearly every Indian around
unfortunately. Took a big part of my business with
them, sorry to say." Danniger turned around, by this
time he had migrated slightly around the shop,
looking at
what the old man had for sale. He turned and faced
the old man, saying "That is a real shame isn't it
now. I'm very sorry to hear the news." He did not
let on how well he knew her, or how close they
were. It was not the greatest disappointment in life,
but it would have been nice to say his goodbyes. It
was just one of the many bumps in the road of life to
him now. He thanked the old man, bought a few 5

cent cigars and left.

He had let go of the old days, he no longer was the boastful youth he was in those days. He had in his own way learned happiness from letting go. He let go of the way things had been, and of all his grasping after things. He was content to allow things to be as they are. The man who knew Weeping Wolf would be distraught, angry, and bitter, but he had passed away. The youthful scout and new cattleman that was grasping, getting and accomplishing had faded with age and experience. As they rode out of the Montana Territory, past the fences of the Ranch, out of the foothills of the Sierra, he became someone else, he became a milder Captain Danniger. He came to accept the towns, railroads, and people that meant the end of what he had known as The West. He knew now, that it was all over. He accepted the fact that the Country was getting closer and closer into him. Montana was not yet a state, but could be soon. The towns and the people they brought squeezed him, but after all what in the world could he do about it? The life he had enjoyed in those passing moments of years gone by was now over forever. As they rode down into the flat lands the fire of desire in him faded out, leaving a man willing to accept things as they are. Weeping Wolf was gone, the quite moments near the fire, the idle chatter in the afternoons, every peaceful afternoon they had together had passed on, and there would be no more. He did not mind though. He did not mind because he had enjoyed it. It was a part of the legacy of his life, once he had lived it, he had it forever. Not that he should hold onto it like a dog holds onto a bone, but hold it like a child holds a pet bird, lightly in the hand, allowing it to come or go as it pleases.

He went back to the little spot where the hands had built camp, it was a couple days ago that he left them, and they would be expecting him. Canso saw him as he came up. They talked briefly, and Canso knew something had happened to his Captain. He did not know what it was, but he knew the old man had experienced something. "Captain, it is good to see you have returned, we have enjoyed our rest. I think it will be good to ride on tomorrow."

Southern Great Plains 1883

"Senor, Senor, we are happy to be out of that horrible place. It was so flat and so cold." Juan said, as they started to see the mixed mesquite scrub land of west Texas. The weather turned remarkably warm as they got closer and closer to home. They had been riding another month since they left the Plains, and the hilly scruff of Texas as a sight for sore eyes. It would not be long before they would part paths, and the Captain would go back to his family, and they would start the rest of their lives.

They had visited the tiny ranch where he got his start as they just got into Texas. The family that had bought it greeted him, unable to believe their eyes. He was as surprised to see the same people he had left over ten years ago. Mr. Beam stood out on the front stoop as they rode in, looking but not being able to believe his eyes. The old scraggly man riding up with the broad white hat was The Captain Danniger that had sold him the ranch so many years before. Beam smiled and greeted the wayfaring strangers as they rode up. They exchanged courtesies and stayed the night. The Captain reminisced about days gone by. He thought about the roughness he and Rebecca endured, and the many arguments they had about everything. They argued about the Ranch, what to do next, and every other thing under the sun. It was all passed now though. He forgot and forgave what had happened over those years, and went on with his life. The Beams were happy to have the place though, dry as it was. They were able to squeeze out a life from the place though.

The next morning it was dusty and the sun fought its

way over the horizon. The puffs and swirls of dust tried to hide the rays of the sun. Mr. Beam and the Captain rose up early, and started a pot of Beam's rot gut coffee. The smell was not the freshest in the world, it was oily, but did have some taste and a caffeine kick. The oily smell soon filled the house and the cowboys were awakened. They were a lively bunch, and talked a great deal, at least among themselves. They filled the house with their loud voices.

The Captain and his cowboys left early and where on their way. They would make a short lunch along the way, or perhaps stop by in some tiny town before parting. The land expanded around them as the red sun slid down behind the tiny hills. Juan spoke up "It will be good to camp. We will eat beans and bacon." Indeed they would eat beans and bacon. Their tired old horses trotted on. The palomino, bay, and orange-brown American Quarter all looked very tired, and the men too were tired. Theirs being an arduous journey, and lucky for the Mestizos, they would not have to repeat it. Diego and Juan were just five-hour's ride from their families. They deserved the bacon and the rest. It had been a long journey. Their Captain would be on his way soon.

"This is a good place." Juan said. There were little dunes and a sandy stream flowed by. They gathered a few sticks of firewood and started up their bacon and beans. After eating they had some small talk. Canso spoke up saying "This is good. This is good enough Captain. We can leave you here now." The Captain was not completely surprised. It was not definite where exactly they would part. He expected Canso to want to go back to his family, but in fact it did not matter much. After they had lived so much together, in Montana, the many trails, through breaking mustangs and all the rest, it seemed that there was not much point in trying to make some dramatic going away ceremony to it. They knew sooner or later this day would come. The cowboys did not see much reason for the Captain to take them all the way to Texas, but if he wanted to, they would allow him. They almost expected for him to turn back at the Beams, but for some reason he did not.

Finally Canso simply thought it was enough. There was little point to making the man carry them all the way. The Captain simply said "Alright then." Looked up briefly from his beans, then leaned back against the sandy bank. They cleaned up camp. Diego and Juan got on their horses and carried on together, they waved their sombreros in the air and pressed the horses on to a slow gallop. Canso, The Captain's main man for so many years stood as they put the cooking equipment into the Captain's bags. They stood and looked at each other. The other cowboys said their quick good byes and left. "Captain. I wish you and your family the best. The best in life. It has been a good life with you." Canso said. "It has been good to see you these many years. I wish you the best." He got on his horse and rode away. It was the end of many things for both men, but also the beginning.

The Captain started his return to the Ranch in Montana Territory, taking two of the horses back as insurance, leaving the others to the Mestizoes as a farewell present. He would be out all alone for another two months kriss-crossing and making his way back to the piney, cold confines of Montana.

Kansas 1883

The Captain had some time for reflection along his route home. Of course to say so may well be to say the obvious. The long, boring plains lay before him, now more boring than ever without his companions. The vast plains were often a place of reflection and introspection, now as the great man strode out on

one of perhaps his last long solo journeys he had
great reason to dwell in the introspection the plains
offered. Now he was starting the end of an era of his
life, he was becoming a new man. He had let go of
the high years of becoming rich and squeezing every
penny out of everything he could. As he trotted past
train depots, villages, and ranches, he noticed how
things had changed. Even way out in Kansas a man
hardly had room to move his elbows without hitting
his neighbour. Civilization had grown up all around
him, creeping up like a wolf on an elk. The West
that he knew was gone, but he reckoned there was
nothing he could do about it. He couldn't keep on
moving west forever because in awhile he'd be in the
Pacific Ocean. He couldn't bring back the old days
when he'd cavort with Mountain Men, riding up
mountains for the Army on scouting expeditions.
Gone were the days he'd go out elking without
seeing a soul. Gone were the great herds of bison,
and the Indians too.

It was getting cold, and the snows would soon be on
them again. It was not sad though, the West
disappearing. He knew now, as an old man that
nothing is forever. All one can do is stay in the
moment, and see it for what it is. The West is not
something he could grab onto and hold like a picture
in a frame. The West was the experience of his life.

He was surprised at how short lived The West really was. He could remember his parents talking about when anything west of the Alleghenies was The West. President Lincoln was considered some backwood bumpkin. He came from Out West, somewhere beyond civilization where nobody knew anything. There he was though, president, and not much more than twenty years later, The West was not The West, and another twenty years would see The West all but disappear.

He reflected on not only his life, but his entire life, the meaning of his life, the ups and downs of his life, and the entirety of what it was or was not. He had been fooling himself for much of his life. The bitter resentment against the Yankees, and the fire of ambition that built in him during the War years was bad medicine indeed. They had made him rich in some ways. He had taken the training on the battlefield and converted that into a way of being a businessman. It didn't mean anything though. He realized this now, now that he had closed down the Ranch, that the hands were gone, and that he would buy no more land, he saw that it did not mean a hill of beans. These things, difficult, long, dirty, dusty, and dangerous, they were empty of inherent meaning. The only meaning they had were those that he bestowed on them

He rode on that way, thinking, and resting for another month. He came back not so much a different man, but the man that he was destined to be. He finally had come to peace with the way things are. He let go of his War time aspirations for money and power, and his life-long pursuit of his destiny. He realized then that destiny is not so much grabbed by you, as you are grabbed by it.

The Fourth Noble Truth
There is a Path Leading out of Suffering

Montana Territory
November 1883

As he got up onto the high plains he could see the
flicker of the lights at home. Finally he left the flat,
low lands behind him. His horses were getting tired,
and he could see their breath jetting out of their
nostrils. It was just getting dark, and the horizon
was a purplish black. It was the purple-black that he
remembered from days passed by. Jenny was most
likely reading one of her silly books. He expected to
be there in another hour. It was getting cold and he
gathered his coat around himself. His broad white
hat was less white now, and while he tried to sit up
straight in the saddle, fatigue had a hold of him and
he would sink back every time he tried to sit up.
"Come on girl." He said to his horse as he gripped
the saddle horn tight and tried to stay upright.

Finally he made it inside the outer fence of the
Ranch and to the front yard. Jenny thought she
heard something and looked out the window. There
was her long lost father, she could not believe it. She

got up and walked to the door, opening it and said "Well hello father, it's nice to see you again." He could not believe his ears, but it was her voice. It had been so long since he heard her and her voice sounded strange to him, like something from another world. In some ways it was another world, he had been among the cowboys so long he had forgotten the ways of women.

"Hello, hello daughter!" He said, much louder than the passive greeting of his daughter. "How are you, long time no-see." He continued. He knew his daughter would always be a creature of a different colour to him. He finally got off his horse and hugged her. He was noticeably dirty and stained from the months on the trail, but it didn't matter to her. She grabbed him, all the same. Rebecca made her appearance now, from behind the doorway Jenny had left standing wide open, letting all the warm air out of the house. She rushed out shutting the door loudly as she came. Jenny took the horses to the barn and started caring for them. He was tired, truly tired and said softly as he embraced Rebecca "I really do love you, you know." They stood there a few short moments, the night gathering around them, the purple shades on the horizon of the mountains turning jet black, the first chilling breezes of winter rushing around them. He knew he was home. He was finally home.

In Town
Spring 1884

"Well you old scudder you, how have you been?"
The Captain asked Schantinger after so many
months. "You still chomping down on the buffalo
are you?" Danniger said loudly, his voice echoing in
the saloon. He moved a few chairs as he made his
way across the room to meet his old friend. "Thank
God it's getting warm again." The Captain
continued. It was just starting to get green outside.
The sky was a bright blue and beautiful. The
mountains could be seen from the windows of the
old weather-beaten saloon. The room had an echo
with its high ceiling and the mens' boots could be
heard thudding as they walked. Schantinger's
movements were jerky, he was still energetic for and
old man. He turned and looked at Danniger as he
made a move toward him. "Ha!" Schantinger
exclaimed, surprised to see old Danniger. "You old
'possum how are you?!" He yelled in return. "You
old dog you, I haven't seen you in a coon's age.
Where in
hell have you been?" Danniger stopped moving now,
and looked at his old friend. "Well, I've been many
places you know." He replied. "Many places indeed"

Captain continued. "And as for you? What have you been doing with yourself these months?"
Schantinger looked at Danniger in turn now saying "Let's take a seat shall we? And we can talk about all your adventures, or should I say our respective adventures in turn."

They sat down with a little whiskey and talked things over. They talked a good long time. They talked about the town, about The West, about their wives, and everything else in between. They talked about how the town was not the same as when they first came, and how it would not be the same after they were dead and in their graves. They talked about the buffalo all but being gone, and the Indians too. They talked about how it seemed that Jenny would never find a husband, the whole valley filled with Swedes, or none. They talked about the sweet beauty of coming to terms with life, or at least what one might tack down as being called life.

After their long talk the men just stopped and sat there. A number of Swedish farmers, old cattle busters, Mexicans, and just regular townsfolk had settled in for a few drinks. The two men looked around them. The mountains could no longer be seen from their vantage point, having been obscured by the throngs of people that had accumulated.

Schantinger had been looking at his whiskey for a while, it stood golden in the glass. He looked up from his drink and said "I guess that's it then. You're not going to be buying up any more land, not at least in these parts." Danniger replied "I guess not. After all, I think it all comes down to that. We all have to stop somewhere and just continue on as we are. A man gets to a point in life when he had done all that he needs to do. Honestly, it's been a good life for me. I don't know about you, but I've had a good life in this town. Might as well enjoy my damn self for a change?"

Schantinger looked up at his friend, his face shiny, his cheeks becoming red and bulging out as he grinned a reply to Danniger's statements. He leaned back in his chair and said "Yep, I guess you're right after all, you old 'possum you."

Civil War: Buddhism in America

Introduction

Buddhism is one of the fastest growing religions in America outside of Islam. Some of this growth is due to immigration by those whose native religion is Buddhism, but some of the growth is caused by those who come to Buddhism by conversion. While Buddhism is a religion known for its peacefulness, there is a civil war of sorts brewing in the mixed environment of Buddhism in America. Buddhism is divided on many fronts, some obvious, some less-so. The obvious first division is between those who have Buddhism as a native religion and those who have taken it on, as they say, with the conviction of a convert, as an adopter of the religion. Besides this, the age-old divisions of Theravada, Mahayana, and Tibetan continue as they have for centuries, and continue their age-old debate in this new-found land.

Myself, a Buddhist American of about fifteen years now, have experienced Buddhism in a variety of forms here. From Zen centres, to Buddhist Churches, to Tibetan groups, to Thai forest monasteries, and suburban Sri Lankan Viharas. There are many places one can practice, learn, and be involved in Buddhism today in the USA. Through my experience, I have noticed all is not completely well within the community of enlightenment seekers.

My motivation in writing this book is not to cause controversy, because I believe the controversy is already there, and simply laying, waiting to be discussed. In my own journey to learn and experience Buddhism, I have come head to head with obstacles of many different types. Some caused by the foreign cultural environment of Buddhism, some by the mixed reception Buddhists can give to new comers.

Buddhism is one great example of the melting pot, or mixed salad of the American cultural experience. It brings out some of the important issues of tolerance, religious freedom, and stereotyping that have been present in America since its very beginning. It can bring out the racism in both the native American population, and the new immigrants bringing it with them. It also opens up issues of language and cultural understanding. America is a land of diversity, integration, and multiculturalism. However, these mixes have, over time been cause for bigotry, racism, and the like.

As I first became a Buddhist and started exploring different groups throughout the US, it became clear to me that language and cultural barriers were very important. This book is in part an expression of some of the troubles and frustration I have had along my own search of Buddhism in America. I remember one Burmese practitioner saying that I mustn't mix techniques. He had finished a temporary ordination and I was giving him a ride to the airport. We discussed our practice briefly and I explained I like to use some parts of many traditions I have come in contact with. He meant that I should not mix meditation techniques of say his sect with those of Goenka, and Zen, or others from the vast assortment available, and practice them at the same time. He suggested I pick just one and use it alone. This is a standard response to many would-be Buddhists, wishing to keep the traditions of their own sect pure. Perhaps he meant for me to follow one of the newly developed meditation schools such as his own or Goenka and follow it alone. In fact none of these new sects is true Buddhism as the Buddha practised. The idea that one should take up one of these new-found traditions, mostly generated within the last hundred years or so, and say one is practising orthodox Buddhism is absurd. This brief conversation that took all of about thirty seconds was the single most important motivation for me to write this book.

It is very common among American Buddhists to mix and match techniques, schools, etc. This after all, is what America is all about (See Stephen

Batchelor and his writings at Tricycle.) Batchelor is himself a character of controversy, teaching what some think is far from orthodox Buddhism. We mix traditions from the old (or in the case of some Buddhist sects not that old) and create our own new, improved and unique version. So as my new Burmese friend was trying to help me in his own way, he showed that he did not really understand what Buddhism in America is about. Is it wrong to mix and match schools of Buddhism? That I believe is a point that can be debated for centuries and never really come to a resolution. The fact is that today no pure school of Buddhism exists. The fact of sects, some of them relatively new wish to keep themselves unadulterated just emphasises the point that Buddhism, especially in America is wrought with schisms, debates, and factions.

In my own search to understand Buddhism, language and culture became obvious obstacles. In some cases it was clear that the Asian Americans I encountered did not want a Caucasian to share in their religion, or their temples' activities. It was their sanctuary where they could be themselves among their own people. Also, trying to understand the broken English of these practitioners made it difficult to understand what was really going on. The religion was enclosed in a difficult to open package of foreign culture, strange language, and concepts difficult to grasp. The philosophy of Buddhism is totally unlike other Western European religions. Stephen Batchelor who is a Western Buddhist teacher who spent time ordained in Asia mentions in his book Confession of a Buddhist Atheist his own cultural and philosophical conflicts. In my own experience, the traditional cultural appendages of ancestor worship, mysticism, folklore, and legend that surrounded Buddhism as I found it caused further misunderstanding.

However, all was not lost and I continued to seek out Buddhism. Buddhism is a logical, practical religion that would appeal to the Founding Fathers of the American Revolution, but yet comes in a foreign culture, and often a foreign tongue. In many cases monks and lay practitioners can barely communicate in English. Also Asian and Asian American Buddhists can have little interest in the real teaching of the Buddha, or in any meaningful practice. Rather, they would like to practice the new traditions which developed when Buddhism was mixed with their indigenous cultures. For the Caucasian American wanting to get the most out of the religion, this can cause all sorts of problems. My own experience has at times been frustrating.

Finding monks or teachers I can communicate with, and finding groups that really want to practice have brought problems. This being said, Americans/Caucasians/etc. Often find themselves segregated either purposefully, or simply by the factors that are, into their own separate groups. There are large Buddhist communities that are almost totally Caucasian. I will discuss this in more detail later.

Many come to Buddhism unknowing of these great divisions, but they do exist. When an American first sees the maroon and ochre coloured robes, smells the incense, and sees the bright flashes of gold-plated Buddhas, it is easy for him to not fully understand what is going on, and often as not, not really care as long as he leaves with good feelings. I write this as somewhat of a study, and somewhat of a conjecture, but at any rate to study an interesting and constantly changing subject: Buddhism in America.

The External Face of Buddhism in America

At first glance, people tend to make assumptions and think how they perceive things to be is how they really are. To start digging into the issues of Buddhism in America, I think it's helpful to give you a short break down of the different groups that practice it here. In the next few paragraphs I will give a short break down of whom is represented by what group(s), and the demographic norms of different groups.

Buddhism in America comes in two large divisions at first glance. While this is not the complete picture, it is a good place to start. The major division is between those groups, centres, temples, etc. that cater mostly to Asians, either Asian Americans, or Expatriate Asians living in America, and those centres, etc. that cater to Caucasian Americans, those of European decent, and other non-Asian practitioners. When I speak of Caucasian Buddhism, I don't mean to exclude the Africans, African Americans, or other members of the non-Asian, non-native, Buddhists who call themselves Buddhist. I mean to describe that part of the Buddhist population that is primarily Caucasian and either a convert to Buddhism or first generation Buddhists.

There are huge, and mostly segregated populations of mostly Caucasian Buddhists. They have come to Buddhism through friends, through a college class, or some other means, but generally are not of Asian decent, and are mostly not born into Buddhism families. They mostly do not mingle with Asian, or "native" Buddhists, but have adopted Buddhism as their religion. These populations are found mostly within the Tibetan groups, in Zen, and in the version of Buddhism that appears in the guise of "insight meditation", and the like.

Among the Buddhists who are mostly Asian in decent and live in America these are generally Thai, Laotian, Burmese, Chinese, Malaysian, Taiwanese, Cambodian and Sri Lankan. This immediately shows a huge component of Theravada Buddhists, but to a lesser degree Mahayana, in the form of Malaysians, Chinese, and Taiwanese. Zen and Tibetan groups are generally populated by Caucasians. Japanese and other Mahayana sects are mostly peopled by those of Asian ancestry and do a mixed sort of practice, some times combining Shinto, ancestor worship and the like. Here are the "Buddhist Churches" that include Koreans, Japanese, and other Mahayana groups that function less in the way that Buddhist monasteries or temples operate, but in someways like a Christian church, and allow Asian Buddhists to be among their own people. Rarely can one find a Japanese American, or Korean American at Zen centres and the like that Caucasians attend. Chinese or Malaysian Americans can be found in numbers at some of the Chan monasteries though. Tibetans, Nepalese, and other Tibetan-type Buddhists either immigrant, or US citizens almost never can be found practising Buddhism in America.

Another interesting, and perhaps unexpected division of Buddhism in America are what I call the Buddha deniers. These are the groups that are Buddhist in everyway but by name. These are mostly peopled by Caucasians, but there are Asians occasionally also. They like the teaching of the Buddha, practice meditation, and the like, but deny that they are Buddhists. I have seen this in at least two major forms. One group adopts Buddhism, particularly meditation, but will never admit to being "Buddhist" and the other claims that Buddhism is just part of some universal truth that all world religions share.

The second group teaches Buddhism as a universal teaching that in fact predates the Buddha and is part of the true nature of the universe. They deny that his hard work under the Bodhi tree, years of self-depravation, and renunciation of his princely life were important in creating a new path and outright religion. Or, in some cases will adopt all the tenants of Buddhism, but deny that they are true Buddhists, sometimes saying they have created something new, or rather say it is part of a sort of a universal teaching. Furthermore, they deny that all the work his followers did in compiling the Suttas was important, but rather write their own manuals and books, saying those are the ones to follow. This is primarily done with the goal of inclusion. Some among this group, as well as others they believe it is important to allow non-Buddhists to practice Buddhism. They claim one can be a Christian and Buddhist, Hindu and Buddhist, Moslem and Buddhist, etc,

etc. because Buddhism does not require that one change one's religion. This is complete nonsense. To practice Buddhism one must take it on wholly, and embrace all the teaching as it was taught. To worship as a Christian, to the best of my knowledge means to accept Christ as one's saviour, and to be born in heaven after death, go to heaven, or what have you. Wishing to become enlightened and to take refuge in the Buddha, Dhamma, and Sangha has nothing in common with Christianity's goals of obeying the commandments, and taking Jesus as one's personal saviour. For these Buddha denier groups, reading the Suttas, as they were written would be to admit the teaching is Buddhism, so they must create their own. Also, some of these Buddhists have come to Buddhism to escape the narrowness of organized religion, or to enjoy the spiritual progress Buddhism offers, but don't consider themselves religious. They use the techniques of Buddhism but deny that what they're doing is religion.

The other, simpler form of Buddha-deniers are those who are "mediators" they take the teaching of the Satipatthana Sutta and practice it, but somehow like to avoid calling themselves Buddhists. In some places this is more blatant than others. In most cases they know it's Buddhism they just don't say so, in other cases the teachers surely know it's Buddhism, but the students may or may not. Here again, these groups attract those who avoid calling themselves religious.

A slight variation of this group is the insight meditation group. These are plentiful and very diverse in the USA. In fact some groups do not openly deny the Buddha, and in fact some realize that it is Buddhism, but the fact that it is Buddhism is somewhat ignored by them. I should say that some groups by stripping the practice of rites and rituals are in fact practising Buddhism in its clearest form.

Insight meditation and all the variations in which it comes are one of the largest Caucasian factions of Buddhism in America after the Zen and Tibetan groups. Insight meditation comes often in the form of large and highly funded retreat centres, and also of local groups that meet at churches, community centres, and the like. This huge population of insight meditation groups love meditation very much, and practice it devotedly, but some how manage to avoid claiming to be Buddhists. Among these ranks we find some very dedicated, and hard-core mediators, and sitting meditation is their forte. This is one of the largest and most significant groups within the Caucasian Buddhist community.

Is any of this right or wrong? Not just right or wrong factually, but right or wrong within the context of what should or should not be. Well, that is very debatable, and I'm not about to claim I can give a definitive answer to this. It simply is the natural evolution of Buddhism in America. Buddhism, in some respect is about getting away from preconceived ideas of what's right and what wrong, or what's real, and not real. I was just reading Geoffrey DeGraff's translation of the Nikaya, and he said that overall, he found the Teaching to be about determining what is a good Kamma, in other words what is conductive to the path of liberation, what a bad Kamma, in other words what is an obstacle to the path, and then conducting yourself accordingly. When we turn to the debate of the state of Buddhism in America, it is not about right or wrong, but making sense of what is.

A Deeper Analysis of the Situation

On the face of it, Buddhism in America is not the happy, peaceful, or progressive religion that it should be. It is in a position where those who are native to it do not welcome the stranger of the new strange land to it, and the strangers of the new land do not accept the strange ways of those who bring the religion. The new American Buddhists feel compelled to create their own new version of it, and the native Buddhists feel sometimes they do not wish to welcome their new neighbours into the group. This is indeed a bleak situation, however this, as with most things is not only what it appears to be. Buddhism in America does have its problems, but is not on the brink of a real civil war. There are many cases of blending both western and eastern Buddhists, and cooperation between many groups. Let's take a closer look though so we can understand all that is going on.

On closer analysis we see that there is one major reason for the major and minor divisions of Buddhism in America, and that is culture. While America is a melting pot of sorts, having spawned spaghetti and meat balls, a mix never to be found in Italy, baseball, a primitive version of cricket, Tex-

Mex food, and many other cultural mixes, language and culture are also sources of misunderstanding, dislike, and even hatred among the many immigrants that call America home. People have a natural tendency to like to associate with people who are like themselves. They grab onto their particular ways of living, ways of thinking, and ways of doing things and don't like to be asked to change or accommodate people different from themselves.

While Americans are turned on by insight meditation, and enjoy it, they don't want to become fluent in Thai, Singhalese, or Japanese to learn it. They don't want to take on Asian cultural norms, or ways of thinking. While many Asians enjoy the economic prosperity America offers, they don't necessarily like the go-go tempo of life, or the materialism that comes with it. Buddhism naturally has brought out some of the natural conflicts that exist throughout the immigrant community in the US.

Buddhism comes from cultures that are very different from the Jewish-Christian culture than has characterized America for the first two hundred years of its existence. Cultures, with all their subtle ways of communicating, all their unspoken values, philosophies, etc. are very important to any group.

Buddhism, coming from an Asian culture places itself unfortunately in a difficult position for the USA to adopt without problems. For main-stream America, Buddhism comes in a very strange package. The language is strange, the habits are strange, the ways of thinking, acting, speaking, talking, eating, etc. are all strange and foreign. Something as basic as how Asians see the world is totally different from Western cultures. Furthermore, as one comes to understand Buddhism, it is really not like other religions at all. It is not about being a part of a congregation, or upholding rules, it is primarily about developing one's mind. It is on some level not something to be learned or understood, but a process through which one changes totally on a psychological level. Buddhism is more than developing a relationship with God, or doing good deeds, it is about absorbing certain truths and becoming them. It is simply not like any other religion, and for someone who does not grow up in it, or in Buddhist culture, it may take years to really understand what it is all about.

I remember over the years as I visited different temples and the like, that my reception varied quite a bit. In some cases the Asians, living in a foreign land, and trying to speak a foreign language treated me with respect, and welcomed me with congeniality, but overall there was little real mutual understanding. In other cases, I certainly could feel that my presence was not appreciated. In almost all cases real understanding, both linguistically and culturally was a problem. While some treated me with a warm welcome, others were indifferent or would rather that I not have visited. Never-the-less, I remained committed to my pursuit of Buddhism, and am here today to write this article.

Americans wanting to learn Buddhism can be as genuine about their aspirations as anyone else. Americans can have resistance to these foreign influences though, and often, on the other hand Asian immigrants come to their temples to avoid the Caucasian hordes they dislike so much in their new land. It goes to show there may be some resistance to having the Caucasian learn about Buddhism. Sure, Buddhism is about tolerance, getting rid of hate, delusion, and the rest, but these are often Buddhists who only go to the temple for special occasions, much like the "born, wed, and dead" Christians who only go to church when they're baptised, married, and are put to rest.

While the particular conditions of Buddhism in America have lead to divisions based on race, culture, and the like, there are plenty of examples of how America has been an environment of mutual understanding, integration, and acceptance. While Caucasian Americans have started their own centres, so as to avoid the language and culture barriers brought by Buddhism, their willingness to accept Buddhism and make it their own represent a true multiculturalism. To cast away the Judea-Christian heritage and accept this foreign religion, even though in their own forms is a major break-through and is an example of willingness to accept the foreign. Many Theravada centres are known for mixing freely with Caucasians. The expat Asians at many Theravada centres have no problem welcoming them in, even though understanding may be difficult at times. The Bhavana Society in West Virginia is a prime example of this, so are many other groups. While I have painted a picture of division, and certainly it exists, there are many examples of how groups do mix races and cultures. In some cases it is rare for Asians to truly push Caucasian away, though it does happen. Often it is not so much a desire to get rid of the white people, but simply to be themselves among their own.

What Will the Americans Do?

Regardless of the cultural rift, Buddhism offers a great deal to America. Americans, being the innovative, intelligent people they are realize that Buddhism is highly valuable to them regardless of its strange appendages, and often choose to adopt it. The issue then comes up of what form will Americans adopt? In order to avoid the cultural and language issues, Americans have created their own forms of Buddhism. Americans have done what comes naturally to them: adopt, adapt, and create. It should be of no surprise that Buddhism was the same. Overall, the American reaction to Buddhism has been to change it and create their own forms, rather than deal with the problems that develop from trying to fit into already established forms.

It would seem that the easiest way for Americans to adopt Buddhism is to make their own forms so they do not have to contend with the cultural and language barriers. In this way American Buddhists can have things their own way. It is much easier to segregate themselves from the Asians rather than try to adapt. Segregation, in many forms has been the main theme of American Buddhism. Each sect, race, nationality, or school each creating its own centres, and staying for the most part among their own. They do not have to try to learn another language, or try to understand a foreign culture. They take the essence of Buddhism and practice it in their own form. As the Dali Lama said "Buddhism is simple, people are complex." So Americans, within their own predominately Caucasian American centres can really get at what the Buddha taught.

The mostly Caucasian groups are visible in a variety of forms. I have already mentioned some of the divisions in the Introduction. There are Zen groups, Buddha-denier groups, and Theravada groups that have taken on all aspects of the Thai tradition, etc, but this is most visible in the insight meditation groups. These groups are totally, or mostly devoid of cultural aspects foreign to Americans. These groups sit and meditate for the most part. They do not have the Pujas, recitations, ceremonies, or ordained teachers of traditional Buddhism. They often do not have Buddha statues, and don't burn incense. They do often understand the meaning of the teaching very clearly, and especially the teaching of the Satipattana Sutta. In this way they get the benefits of Buddhism, at least the insight and spiritual benefits, without the strange language and culture.

Also, Americans have created their own Zen and Tibetan groups which do come in mostly Asian forms, with chanting, recitations, and ceremony, but are hybrid forms and are attended mostly by Caucasian Americans. In this way Americans can have Buddhism on their own terms.

So American Buddhism, true, American developed Buddhism is not really a melting pot where everyone is the same, but much more like a mixed salad. Many different schools and sects have developed in the US, much like the Asian sects that developed after the death of the historical Buddha, following the historical developments of Theravada, Mahayana, and Tibetan schools all having different teachings, different ways of practising. Now the Americans have their own Buddhism, which is as true as any form of Buddhism, and in fact, at least according to some, a more true version, devoid of the cultural and traditional hang-ups that Buddhism can have in Asian temples, monasteries, and the like. In this way a new American Buddhism has been created, not in a pure new form, but as a hybrid, adopted and melded version of the original.

Now, I have made many assumptions about how Buddhism is and is not represented. I realize there are always exceptions to my research. I'm sure somewhere there is a Tibetan centre in the US that is teeming with expat Asians practising. I have yet to find them in numbers though. Also, notably in the Ajahn Chan monasteries of Abayagiri, and small Thai temples, and other Theravada ones often Caucasians can be found. Among Zen centres, certainly Japanese can be found, but not in numbers.

This begs the question who am I to make all these statements, when obviously there are exceptions to every rule? It is because I want to get to the heart of what Buddhism is, and especially to get to the heart of what Buddhism in America is. Overall, Buddhism is a great religion that offers a lot. Americans, being the innovators they are would naturally adopt Buddhism for the benefits it offers, but are not necessarily all that keen to adopt Asian culture and ways of doing things. Buddhism, being foreign to the Christian ways upon which the United States was founded, has some problems. There are many cultural hang ups, racism, and good old-fashioned misunderstandings that result from such a mix. There can be lack of mutual goals and understanding among the Asian immigrant population, and a true lack of common values also. For the most part what Caucasian Americans want out of Buddhism is meditation and understanding of life. All the other odd bits like chanting, reciting things, precepts, ceremonies, incense burning, etc. are foreign and not necessarily desired by Caucasian Americans.

What Does Buddhism Say About This Sort of Situation?

While I believe it important to make a sort of cultural analysis of Buddhism in America, and any student of Buddhism will benefit greatly from looking at the situation, this information remains mostly academic, and does not really help the student much. Of course there are cultural problems when a foreign religion is brought into a country, the important question is what does it mean to the practitioner.

The important analyses are not so much of all the particulars in regards to the culture of American Buddhism, but rather what the teaching of the Buddha has to say about the culture of American Buddhism. I intend to write much more than simply a summary of Buddhism in America. In fact I believe it very important as a Buddhist to make sense of all the issues, and bring them into the Buddhism context. How does Buddhism deal with conflicts, and what do the conflicts tell us about the nature of the human mind?

Honestly, I have written this essay about this very

topic, what the Buddha would say about this, that is the segregation of the groups of American Buddhism, and how the issues present in American Buddhism relate to what Buddhism is really about. While it is important to set down the circumstances of this dialogue, it is more important to look at the real details of what Buddhism in America means to Buddhism. Buddhism is about getting beyond views, beliefs, traditions, ceremonies, attitudes, etc. Buddhism is not about maintaining traditions, or memorization. Buddha was a revolutionary, a seeker, and a changer. I will discuss more about this later.

The problems plaguing Buddhism in America drive forth the point of the importance of good practice for a Buddhist. Buddhism was created in order to solve human problems. The factions and cult-like behaviour ARE of course human problems. Seeing these problems, as American Buddhists we of course should look deeper at the underlying reasons for them, and work deeper into our practice as individuals. These schisms merely point to the problems we have as people wanting to not really practice equanimity, but rather to make judgements, see our way as the right way, and to make discriminations against those that don't see things our way. The problems with American Buddhism are simply a signal to American Buddhists to see the delusions they have created and in fact reenforce in many cases. At the end of the day Buddhism is about understanding and dealing with exactly these kinds of problems. So, in fact it is an opportunity to learn, and progress within the practice.

Another important issue in studying the evolution of Buddhism in America is the question of if Buddhism is culturally linked. Does American Buddhism point to some important anthropological, or sociological issues present in Buddhism itself? Or is it simply a result of the environment of America? Would Buddhism have been Buddhism outside of an Asian country, the particular time period it started, or the family in which it was begun? Or if Buddhism were started in another area of the globe, would it have developed differently? These are all important questions. Does Buddhism require an Asian point of view, or would it have developed regardless of the circumstances, because as some claim, it is universal knowledge?

I would say it is safe to say Buddhism would most likely not have come about in the way it did, or exactly in the forms that it did, without the particular set of circumstances which surrounded the life of the historical Buddha, and then those who developed the various sects of Buddhism. So while in someways the culture of Buddhism is linked with its time period, Buddhism does have a life outside of those circumstances. Buddhism is culturally linked, but not culturally dependent. It is unlikely that it would have developed outside of Asia, and particularly outside of the religious dialogue of the time. The historical Buddha was just one of many, many seekers in India at the time. The seekers that he studied under were numerous, and you can read about them in the Suttas. Many gurus of the time were meditating, experimenting with different life styles, trying mediation in many, many forms. It was just because of some circumstances that he was able to not only find enlightenment, but also found a new religion. Without the spiritual study in India at the time, none of it ever would have happened. Many of these seekers, like Buddhist monks today were totally dependent on their followers. This culture of gurus, students, and respect for this type of spiritual journey made Buddhism possible.

As well as the cultural benefits of ancient India for Buddhism, there were also problems. The Hindu system of caste is something that the Buddha as adamant against. The culture of Brahmanism, where some are born better than others, and certain work, social position, etc. is dictated by birth were all directly attacked by the Buddha. This clash gave the Buddha a rich environment to make himself different from all the rest of what people were doing. In this way he addressed the social problems of the day. Here, in America today Buddhism is not addressing social problems but finds itself embroiled in immigrant/native born cultural clashes. Like the historical Buddha clashed with Brahmanism, American Buddhists and Asian Buddhists should not cloister themselves only among themselves, but should reach out to find the common ground all Buddhists have.

Now, today, the many Asian countries that Buddhism calls home are not ancient India, and the cultures of those places are most certainly different from that of the historical Buddha. So while the foundation of the religion was dependent on the set of circumstances of the time, it is not dependent on that particular culture to survive and continue. Where does that really leave us though? As a living religion, we can see that it does exist outside of its original circumstances, so it can adapt. Much of the teaching of the Buddha is about getting out of old, entrenched ways of thinking, so it follows naturally that Buddhism can be adopted in a variety of different places. So why then is there the American Buddhist Civil War? It's because people are not deep enough in their practice, and it's easier to hold onto one's cultural norms than to really try to practice. So, it just so happens that this cultural clash between ease and west is the perfect thing to bring out the best practice in all concerned. Those who choose to do things their own way, exclude those different than themselves, and the like might as well not even call themselves Buddhist.

Is it Un-American to be Buddhist?

I was reading "Tricycle" online magazine not too long ago and the subject of Buddhism in America, American Buddhism etc. came up among the discussion pages. The question was not exactly what I have brought up here, but does have some similarities. The question is if it is un-American to be Buddhist. I remember when I was studying at the School or Oriental and African Studies in London that the conflict between modernization and Buddhism in Thailand is very important. There, they asked if it's possible to be a good Buddhist and enter the modern era. For many Thais as they pick up Western culture, and to a certain extent values, it becomes clear that the fast pace and consumerism of the modern age is in many cases in direct conflict with Buddhism.

I know for certain that as Buddhism developed in America certain cultural conflicts occurred between the Asian trappings of the religion and the culture of Americans. As a result Americans created their own centres, etc. As we get deeper into the issues we must realize that not only is it possible that there is a conflict between the peoples' cultures, but also between the culture, or rather the tenants of

Buddhism and American (or even modern Asian nations') culture.

The point of the "Tricycle" debate was that Americanism means to live in consumerism, and to be Buddhism is not. As the discussion developed people mentioned that it is not right to condense the meaning of either of these things into such simple terms. However, like in the case of modern Thailand, one does notice that Buddhism does command that one's values not be those of what would seem to increasingly be the majority of people. So while Buddhism is not anti-consumption, and Americans certainly are known for consumption, it is childish to say one is not possible with the other. What has happened, and what will continue to happen is a dialogue and discussion between Buddhism and its followers, and among the various followers themselves. Americans will certainly develop their own forms of Buddhism, and Asians will continue to work out compromise to allow Western ideas in.

So What Would the Buddha Do?

As I've said earlier, Buddhism is not about
upholding traditions, nor holding onto ideas, views,
opinions, and the like. (Handful of Leaves Vol I pg.
155, Mulapariyaya Sutta). So therefore, it would
seem that all the forms in which Buddhism takes
place in America might be wrong ones. The Buddha
instructed us to lose our views and opinions and
here in America all the Buddhists are latching on
tight to their view, preferring one interpretation of
the Teaching over another. I have no doubt that the
Buddha would have recognized the issues that effect
American Buddhism and would see it as a
opportunity to go deeper with practice.

The issues brought out by Buddhism in America
drive home the human aspects of any human
endeavour, and certainly those human activities that
are sociological in nature. The issues of Asian
Buddhists not understanding American culture, and
Americans not wishing to accept Asian cultural
norms to practice Buddhism merely emphasise the
point that no person is perfect. More than that, by
looking at the sociological, cultural, and
psychological reasons for the rifts in American
Buddhism, we are given yet another opportunity,

given that we are Buddhists, to practice. We are called to escape our narrow mindedness, lack of sympathetic joy (piti), and ultimately the lack of strident practice that allowed the Historical Buddha to become enlightened. The issues of sectarianism are opportunities to see the frailty and imperfectness of the human condition, much in the way that the Historical Buddha saw the ultimately undesirable conditions of human life.

Buddhism does not judge, nor does it fall into false realities, based on self-centeredness. It does not reject anyone because of language, or culture. It does not say we know better than you. In fact the Buddha asked that we question everything he said. During the time of the Buddha, and especially in the past say two hundred years there have been those who are Buddhist, but like to discriminate because of tiny inflections of the Teaching. They for example watch the abdomen during meditation, or watch the whole length of the breath, or scan the body, or only draw attention to the feet during walking meditation, ignoring the rest of the legs, or any number of tiny aspects of practice. All of them claim that they are correct and others are incorrect. They have interpreted the Satipathana Sutta correctly, and all others incorrectly. This is simply wrong in the eyes of the Buddha. The Buddha set down clear rules as to how meditation was meant to be. Then people started cutting it up and giving their own advice on what was the best way to do it. This is utter nonsense.

This study of Buddhism in America shows the falsehoods that people create. It shows the problems of holding onto views, of discriminating. Especially the trap of the ego, all these groups grab onto their methods and traditions saying they are right and others wrong. This is totally wrong. This is the perfect environment to see how Buddhism really works. These Buddhist groups separated by culture and language naturally as humans gather around what is familiar to them and drive away all that is not. They do not really practice, but find it better to do what human psychology dictates and create their own micro-societies and stick to them.

The fact that Buddhism in America is so fragmented goes to show that people will be people no matter what, except for those select few who chose to take the Teaching on and make the best of it. Of course as I've said before there are plenty of examples of where American Buddhists are integrated, Asians, Caucasians, Theravada Buddhists, Mahayana, etc. etc. are all intermixed and do not segregate themselves. Still, for the purpose of this book, we should look at what Buddhism has to teach about sectarianism. The Buddha would obviously not be happy with what had developed out of his Teaching. However, he would most likely not be surprised either. All this infighting and factionist behaviour is just part of human nature, it is just a part of the practice, it's just a shame in America it seems to have gone so far. I believe this is exactly the attitude the Buddha would take.

There are a few key points about Buddhism that come up when one analyses Buddhism in America. The main goal behind Buddhism is to become enlightened. Now, saying that in and of its self does not make much sense. Trying to define or explain enlightenment is nearly impossible, even for the enlightened. Enlightenment is certainly a specific state of mind, which has many characteristics. The issue is that all the segregation, entrenchment, and other ways of exclusion are very much against what Buddhism teaches, are keeping those who practice them off the path to enlightenment. It may be easier for groups to stay among themselves, but it does not do their practice any good in the long run. Furthermore, it shows a fundamental delusion, or in other words, unenlightenment on the part of those doing it. It is easy to exclude those who disagree with you, not easy to really practice the Teaching.

Now, I know there are many reasons now days to discriminate between false Dhamma and real, however this is not the issue I am speaking about, this day in age it is important to discriminate between legitimate and illegitimate teachers. Just to clarify, I think it's a good idea to simply list some of the particular faults that arise when we practice sectarianism. Let me list the areas that cause problems for Buddhism in America.

Ego centre

At the heart of the issue of "us against them" or of "We are right, they are wrong." which presents itself in the guise of different groups separating themselves, and putting themselves up as a standard of correctness is ego-centeredness. These are all wrong according to Buddhism. They stop a person from using the principle of Ehepassiko. They prevent one from doing the constant reality checking and personal introspection so important to Buddhism. Using this line of thinking lulls one into a false sense of rightness, and dulls the intellect so vital to Buddhism. In this case people tend to be idle and stop working on the path. Once they have found a group they are comfortable with they simply go along, following like sheep. They no longer bother to question if they are doing right or not.

Another part of this is why in many cases Buddhists in America have segregated themselves. The Thai groups don't attend the Tibetan, and the Caucasian insight meditators don't attend the groups of the Sri Lankans, and etcetera. The ego saying "We're right, you're wrong." is at the foundation of why these Buddhist groups don't mix. This shows a fundamental fault in the practice of these groups. While being focussed on one particular path is good, they have done it for the sake of not bothering themselves from the hard work of seeing what's right and what's wrong. Stopping the discovery process is against the Buddhist principles of searching. Sociological pressures of inclusion and clan ties have trumped following the Path.

Egoism is at the heart of what the Buddha was against. The ego clouds our judgement, makes us think we are things we're not, and makes it impossible to realize the teaching of the Buddha. Egoism is easy though. In most cultures, and especially American, we are encouraged to be egoists, we are encouraged to build walls around ourselves and include those like us, and exclude those who are different. It is so much easier to assume we are right and everyone else wrong. We don't have to do any really hard work then.

Reality check

Throughout the enlightenment path of the historical
Buddha, he was constantly checking his method, and
counter analysing it with those of his contemporaries
(Handful of Leaves Vol I Thanissaro Bhikkhu 33).
Making constant checks on reality, that is to say, as
the student trains he must always check to see if he
is really progressing, and if his progress is authentic.
Those who divide themselves into Buddhists of this
sort or that no longer need to check and see if what
they are doing is authentic Buddhism. In fact many
people prefer the versions of Buddhism they have
created over the centuries than the real thing. As
Buddhism developed the cultures that adopted it
changed it to meet their own particular ways of thinking.

So here, in America the many sects of Buddhism
both new and old have often abandoned the reality
checks of the founder for something that is easier.
By doing this they no longer question what they're
doing or why.

Questioning

Those who don't question what they're doing, or
question their position on their spiritual path don't

do well as Buddhists. By separating into different groups it takes the pressure off people to do the real work. The Buddha asked that his student continue to question themselves, and question their progress, but not become over involved with it. It is a healthy practice to question what is going on, and what not. He said ultimately we are to be our own masters (Dali Lama), and we should not accept anything he said without proving it to ourselves. A monk at the City of Ten Thousand Buddhas once said during a retreat that we should "Ask ourselves what is real, and what is not." A monk from the Chanmaya tradition told me once also that "I'm becoming more convinced that what we think it real is not." We should continue to question at all stages.

For a Buddhist, when we stop this introspection and questioning of what is real and what is not, we cheat ourselves spiritually. We no longer are the revolutionary enlightenment seekers that the Buddha inspired during his life time, but those simply wanting to take space up within a congregation. We don't understand what the Buddha was about, and we don't allow ourselves the difficulty of really practising. So we lose the depth and meaning of the practice.

Views, opinions

Buddhism is about getting rid of pre-conceived views, opinions, and values. To enter onto the Path means to abandon the ways of the world, and to come to understand how things really are, free from all the views, ideas, and opinions our background, upbringing, etc. impose on us. Holding onto views is a sure way to stunt one's spiritual growth and postpone enlightenment. The Buddha was opposed to views and opinions because they kept one from opening one's mind to the expansiveness of enlightenment. To hold onto one view necessarily means one must abandon another. To hold one opinion of something, most of the time means one has shut out the possibility of any other option.

In fact our views are what bring us to rebirth. As our delusion grasps us in this direction and in that, we are forced to perpetuate our lives on and on further in order to satisfy our wants. Also, because the many factions of Buddhism in America grasp onto their views they never get to the development of insight needed to attain enlightenment (Handful of Leaves Vol. I 155) Now, along the path one does learn the right view, and wrong view, one gathers right opinions and abandons wrong ones. To say to hold any opinions or views as a Buddhist is wrong. For the sake of American Buddhism, what I see is a

215

tendency for groups to gather around their own opinions and view of things and reject all others. The separation of this faction and that, according to cultural, historical, and national lines is simply the human tendency to grasp onto views and opinions. This of course is a major obstacle to any true fact finding along one's spiritual journey.

In American Buddhism views and opinions come in the form of the many sects of Buddhism we find. Some groups firmly hold onto the view that they are not Buddhists when the are, some claim to be authentic Buddhists when they aren't, and of course the Mahayana and Tibetan claim that the Bodhisattva way is the only one. America, the land of the immigrant naturally has a tendency for groups to form along ideological lines. Buddhism is about getting beyond these views and opinions, and there is no greater training ground to do so than America. In Asia one would tend to only see Buddhists of one's own type, save in Singapore where all the types meet. Therefore, the American Buddhist has a rich opportunity to see his views and opinions and work them out.

Conclusion

Buddhism in America is complex. It is a result of the history of the country, and the social developments it has experienced over time. Buddhism in America is much an immigrant's tale. The tale of coming into a land of promise and opportunity but finding out, it's not everything you read about in the brochure. Immigrants have often created their own communities, so they can preserve their culture and social systems, and so they have in American Buddhism. They do invite outsiders in though. Just as any Anglo is welcome in the Italian neighbourhoods of America, the many sects of American Buddhism to welcome each other. What would America be, if no immigrants welcomed their newly arrived neighbours? It wouldn't be America!

American Buddhism is a mix of new Buddhism created from borrowed bits of the old, immigrants keeping to their own, and mixes of Americans and immigrants. That, for the most part is what America is, and overall Buddhism has done well in America and will continue to do so. America has much to offer Buddhism, and Buddhism has much to offer America. While the Buddhist path has its troubles in

America, overall it will continue to grow and become better for it.

Zen and the Street Musician

Chapter I
Explanation
Is the Child Father of the Man?
College

Chapter II
The Entry of Zen
The Teachings of Zen

Chapter III
Zen and Artists, Zen and This Artist
A Sense of Purpose
The Artistic Sentiment
Zen as Opposed to the Artistic Sentiment

Chapter IV
The Street Musician Enters
The Birth of the Street Musician

Chapter V
What does Buddhism Have to do With Life , and by
the Way What does Art Have to Do With Life?
Conclusion

" A special transmission outside scriptures. No dependence on words and letters; direct pointing to the mind of man. Seeing into one's nature and attaining Buddhahood."

Bodhidharma

Introduction

At the twenty-first century marches on, we have found Buddhism to still be far from mainstream, but also not as exotic or bizarre as it once was. Since the 1960's the world has become increasingly globalized, and everyone, nearly everywhere has the great opportunity to experience the Buddha's teaching. Call it Dharma, Dhamma, or what have you, it is mostly pure and one of the most revolutionary and important developments the world has ever experienced. This story is that of a young American man growing up in this post-industrial era, who by his own great luck come to know the Dharma. I start with a short episode from his grade school playground days.

"Hey you. You, you little jerk!" He said as he pushed his way through his assembled classmates. He then kicked Jack in various parts of his body. Jack attempted to get away; tripping and stumbling. They were about ten, it was a crisp and cloudy September day. Classes had started about a month earlier. They were assembled outside the cafeteria, our hero had just heard about who it was that had been spreading the rumours. "What do you think you were doing you jerk. Saying all that stupid stuff.

I don't love Mrs. Huttner!" He kicked little Jack Dempner in the butt and legs from the entrance of the cafeteria to half way across the basketball court which also served as a parking lot outside of school hours just in front of the cafeteria. His blows were not the precise ones of a prize fighter, but rather like the wild flaying of an enraged animal, it was more out of rage than planning that he kicked. Jack had been spreading the rumour that our hero loved their teacher for a couple weeks now. Now Jack was a little weeny of a kid; always poking fun, making jokes, ridiculing, all that normal kid stuff that most kids do, or at least a certain percent of kids do on average. Our future street musician had put up with enough of it, it was the last straw. Enough is enough. He was a basically laid-back child; our future street musician. He did not want to push anyone out, ridicule them, or create any bad feelings. Jack on the other hand was driven by a desire to be top dog, make others look up to him. Even though he was a sort of nerd, still Jack was socially advanced enough that he had enough draw potentially to have mass popularity. Jack had his own problems: A childhood lack of confidence, unhappiness with life, and desire for more attention.

Our hero was a quiet child, mostly interested in his own thoughts, his creations in music and wood, and the garden that he and his father kept. He was the classic introverted genius, able to understand himself, but others were an entirely different matter. It would be years before he, like the Buddha before him realized at the end of the day it is one's own mind that determines one's life, but the seeds were already planted. He did not talk much to the other kids, he did not have a good reason to; at least that he could think of at the time, as he struggled to understand the world around him and the people in it. There was too much going on internally, too much figuring out, analysing, observing, learning, seeking, and struggling. At the time he did not know it, but his journey had already begun; the journey to become a street musician and Zen master. His internal searching had started and it would lead him unendingly toward his destiny.

We all start somewhere. Childhood is the beginning of most people's lives, though John Denver claims that life started later on for him. Early on, our future street musician knew that things would be different for him. While at the age of ten he did not know the distances and depths that his life journey would take, he knew that life was a struggle. He did not relate to the other children. Most of them were a waste of his time. Most of them did not have much interest in him. He felt in someways a desperation to make friends, to be one of the crowd, but then again, saw the crowd as a bunch of losers. His story began with conflict; an internal seeking, asking, and wondering. Always comparing and analysing, figuring out; coming up with answers. He was very young and green still, but in time he would come into his own.

On one hand he was content to allow Jack just to keep up with the nonsense because after-all that is all it is, nonsense. Our hero didn't really see much point in starting trouble, but he did see a point in getting Jack off his back. Our future street musician wanted to be himself and be left alone; but no one can be alone forever, eventually we must all make our way in the world. Even the ancient Taoist masters, living on the mountains of ancient China had to come out into life inside the world, and out of their own minds, imaginations, and personal mental conditions, dealing with all the internal conflict present in any spiritual seeker.

So there he found himself in a person-to-person conflict, fighting back in order to get Jack back for the constant assaults. It was not something he sought out, but the situation found him. The journey began.

Chapter I

Explanation

In life most of us at some point ask "why". While some spend their whole lives entangled in the myriad of activities we engage in: raising a family, seeking fame and fortune, or any of a number of different activities. While many are locked in this constant doing without asking, many stop to see what exactly is going on around them. For some eventually they stop and, in some way or another ask themselves "Who am I, why am I here, what does it all mean?" We may not say it in those terms, but we all have the opportunity in life to wonder about these most fundamental questions. Some of us do it out of desperation, some do it out of some strong spiritual yearning. Our street musician will do the same.

I have written this little story to explain things. Of course there are a great many things that can be explained, but at least explain a little something about one of the most important things that can be explained; to put in perspective the life of one man, in the context of the Buddhist tradition, and shed some light on Zen in the modern American context as well as how it refers to our "hero's" life. To put the Buddhist tradition in the context of one man's life so as to help the lives of all people everywhere through practice of the Buddhist path, and obviously improve the lives of the readers of my little tale. To demonstrate how one person can apply the Buddha's teachings to his life, through the wonderful, satisfying, and ultimately relieving empirical learning, testing, seeing, and proving that is the heart of what the Buddha taught. It is only through first-hand experience that we come to understand the Buddha's teachings.

Never from reading, or hearing the teaching will one become enlightened. Only through the tough work of clearing out the mind, freeing one's self of all the mental pitfalls and barriers does one become free. One must sweat the white beads, strain and toil under one's own negative past karma. This is the only way. It is not all bad though, because in some ways it is a paying back of what is owed, and evening of the energies of the universe. It is only through fire that a sword becomes ready for battle, only through crushing pressure that a diamond is formed. It is through this glorious process of self-help, self-observation, and self-realization that each and every Buddha or Bodhisattva, becomes awake, becomes enlightened.

This story, as all stories are on one level or the other are, is a story of LIFE. An explanation of life, a sample of life, or an aspect of life. What is life though? While we talk about life, around life, and through life, this does not answer what it is. It is nearly impossible to define. Sure, science has its answers, but so much of it is still hidden in mystery. Religions, philosophies, and the like have claimed to know the meaning of life for eons. Life for the Buddhist, especially a human life is the opportunity to become enlightened and help others do the same. Within Zen and Buddhism in general we require a human life to become enlightened. A godly life is too pleasant, the life of an animal too coarse, only in the human context is intelligence mixed with the limits of an earthy life. It is as simple as that. This particular story, and particular life is one of a man on a serious and heart-rending life's journey.

Every story from Great Expectations to Jaws is at some level basically about life. While writers say that conflict is what drives plot, plot in my mind is almost always on some level about LIFE; exploring it, being involved in it, soaking up the drama of it. We are so involved with life and its details; we cannot help but be drawn into it. I think only the hard core scientists can devoid their work of some aspect of human life. Only the true mathematical genius, or laboratory dwelling chemist does not need the human context to make sense of his work. Doctors, lawyers, actors, stock brokers, tea salesmen, plumbers, professors, and tire manufacturers all deal in some aspect of humanness that would not exist if not for the characteristics and components of human life as we know it. In this particular case, for our street musician, and for Zen practitioners life is a training ground, a test, an opportunity. Life for those on a spiritual path is usually looked on as a combination of these things, but basically is very good fortune, or even a gift from heaven. Life is indeed many things, it can be difficult and trying, can be horrible even, and often is. Life can be joyous to, wonderful, perfect, but really in the end it is what you make of it, it how you relate to it; and nothing more.

The story of a person's life, or LIFE (the single universal life connecting all individual lives as related by many of the world's religion), is nothing more than fruition, the ripening of activities, both physical and psychological. Many of the world's religions consider this particular experience of having a body, personality, job, etc. is part of an interconnected LIFE, a life which is connected to each and every other thing. The separation between "you" and "I" is an artificial one that we have created. Life, for those on the spiritual path is an experience of interconnectedness, of getting to know one's self and how that self interrelates to the world. It is an experience of learning, growing, and becoming who we really are. In the case of the Buddha the psychological is the most important, because as stated in the Lotus Sutra "Everything is made of mind" for the follower of the Buddha's way. We live in our minds so to speak. Everything in regards to personal growth occurs in the psychological sphere. We create our personalities in our minds as we process and interact with all we see and experience. Our ideas of whom we are, are really all just in our minds. Getting to understand our minds is one of the greatest fundamentals of the Buddha's teaching.

Don't misunderstand me, the Buddha's practice is a psycho-physical one, very much so. As with the Yogic and Vedic masters that he, the historical Buddha studied with, adopting, and adjusting their practices and teachings to create his own; the body is used as a tool to the enlightening of the mind. Not the simplistic, logical mind that Freud, Kant, and Jung got to know so well, learning about the nooks and crannies of the psyche, but the real, deep, mind that is so tied to the body it is inseparable. This is the mind both a part of our animal essence, but also of our supra mundane consciousness.

According to many Buddhist masters this fruition of experience and mind is the SAME fundamentally for every sentient being that comes into this existence as we know it. Every being is bound to realize Nirvana, it may be a few eons, but the cycle of birth and death is only broken by this realization. Each and every sentient being will continue through births and deaths until the ultimate enlightenment is achieved. That is to say that while obviously the particular experiences of each life are different, the main realizations are identical for each being. A release from the ego, realization of dependant origination, wisdom, and deep compassion all comes about. This ripening is called enlightenment and is not the choice of only those who claim the Buddhist path as theirs, but rather a requirement of the great blessing of being born into a sentient body on this place we call earth. According to some Tibetan traditions, regardless of one's spiritual
practice everyone eventually becomes enlightened. This is most likely how the historical Buddha understood things, after a few decades of hard spiritual practice. For the Buddha it was enlightenment that we all find eventually, for the Hindu, the religion from which he came, it was the supra-soul, because this is basically the teaching of Hinduism, that heavens and hells exist, and there is a plethora of different bodies to be in, different lives to

live, but we all come home eventually to the supra-soul, that is one with God, one with everything, and really one with whom we are.

Enlightenment is home, it is where we rightly belong. Not that it is a physical place, but it is where our true nature abides deeply and richly. Enlightenment, according to those Tibetan scholars is where every sentient being at some point in time MUST stop, with out it these beings would continue to whirl around with out end in samsara. Sooner or later each and every being after accumulating enough positive energy, enough merit, enough wisdom, compassion, etc. is lucky enough to come to know the teachings of the Buddha, so that he, she, or it can finally and blissfully come "home" to abide in the state that is their birthright, nirvana.

So what you ask? Indeed, I agree, all this sort of highfalutin talk is nice, and very true, but what does it matter? What good is all this knowledge and theory with out any body on the bones? So here enters our street musician. In this tale I would like to exemplify a Buddhist life for a Buddhist man, to tell his tale so as to make some sense of all this talk of Buddhas and samsara, and enlightenment. High talk is good, but it is of no value unless it can be applied to our lives. Makes it a little more human doesn't it?

Is the Child Father of the Man?

It's hard to say if anyone ever has a "perfect" childhood. Many claim to, or like to say they know those who have. Childhood is when we lay the foundation of our ego, it is when we discover for the first time who we are, and who everyone else is in relation to ourselves. For our hero, childhood to him seems to be not perfect, but nothing special. He has considerable suffering, and it is apparent early on that he is not like any of his fellow classmates. We, like him have our first loves, our first hates, our first "real" experiences that we create ourselves without the help of mom or dad. We discover that life is not always we might think it is or wish it was.

Our street musician starts out as any other human does - a child. He starts out early loving to play music, and loving to spend long hours alone. He thinks that music is a good choice in life, but does not put a great deal of energy into the decision. We have to ask ourselves does his childhood dictate what the rest of his life will be like? This is any issue that he must deal with, and most certainly will deal with as time goes on. It's easy to put words in people's mouths, to assume what they mean, and the like. For our to-be street musician, it is best to let him do what all decent men would do, and speak for himself:

"For me, childhood was a mostly unpleasant thing. Filled with great expectations, angst, joys, pleasure and pain. Relatively early in childhood is was quite clear to me that I was not like any other of the children. I seemed to stand out. My interests, my ideals, they were different. The other kids also noticed I was different. I was never asked to join any one's team, always the odd one out, the one ignored during recess. I began to wonder why, why me?'

Sort of rough isn't it? Life is hard for our little guy, at least early on. The school yard kicking episode is maybe just a fruition of some negativity. Well, our hero is maybe not all that special, because few people would really say they have a perfect childhood.

What exactly is childhood? I think this is a valid question at this point. In many ways Zen is about asking what in the world things are, and how we relate to them. Childhood, is on its face the time from when we are born to when we are adults, but what does that mean? Childhood, as most things can really only be defined and understood in context. The most important aspects of childhood, as far as my purposes are: socialization, the creation of the ego, the beginning of questioning "Who am I?", And experimenting in what "I" can and cannot do. We leave our mothers' arms and go out to see the world. We make our first friends, start to learn all the ins and outs of human society, and get to know our own personality traits. We begin to think of ourselves as separate individuals, with characteristics all our own. We begin to wonder what in the world does it all mean, why was I born? Who am I? From the time we make our first step, to when we say our first word, then fly our first plane or convict our first felony, we are on a journey, and the basics of this journey begin in childhood, when we begin to learn, sometimes painfully who we are, who society is, and what is possible in the world.

So our future street musician is now a young, budding ego, already begun to differentiate "me" from "you". What he did, thought, and was, in RELATION to what others did, thought, and were. Interesting? What does Zen have to say about this? What is the relationship of Buddha's teachings to this?

The ego, in the egotistical language of everyday life, is the artificial separation of "you" from "me", is of course a natural convenience in daily speech. We do after all live in different bodies, our organisms are different. For the sake of understanding each other we must use these terms. The ego that we construct all around us makes life difficult though. The way the ego gets in the way of our spiritual progress is all very, VERY serious. This ego-centered approach to life, the Buddha said was utter and complete nonsense. So for the normal person childhood is in many ways the overture to adulthood. The child IS father to the man, but childhood for many is also father to future Buddhas and Bodhisattvas. So it is in childhood that we have the opportunity to first learn who we are, but also who we are not. Our childhoods very much do make us who we are as adults, but this is only part of the picture. We have the choice to see through the delusion of our conditioning early in life (assuming we are not so lucky as the historical Buddha, and others to not acquire the standard delusions most of us do in childhood, the Buddha as you may know was shielded from the harsh realities of life by his father), and use it as a tool in our path to enlightenment.

As a Buddhist, every second is in fact father to the next, and each in a way is a rebirth. One thought, action, volition, idea, or inaction leads surely, completely, and unanimously to the future, so that we bit by bit create our reality through free choice. Children, and their actions are the fathers to the adults they become. While they may not know it, it is true. Our future street musician has already begun his introspective journey.

"I don't know, Adam." Our hero says. "I'm not so sure if that's a good idea to shoot your neighbor's dog with the bee-bee gun." It was a hot August day, and school would be starting again soon. The two twelve-year-olds were enjoying the last days of Summer at Adam's parents farm. "It seems to me every creature ought to have the opportunity to live a good life, all by himself, without being shot with bee-bees." He says, trying to dissuade Adam. By that time the old mangy Cocker-mix turned and scampered back up the creek bed and disappeared. Adam said, "Oh, I was just teasing anyway. You know I'd never hurt old Bingy."

The boys were fast friends, though as puberty set in they would part. They shared many a lazy Summer day, skipping rocks, fishing with home-made fishing gear, and generally being boys. They formed their own secret society, and talked about spaceships, and going to the moon, and how to survive in the wilderness alone. It was a happy friendship, but would not last. It was just a childhood bond that would not stand the test of time.

Our street musician has already begun to wonder why, how, how come, why me, why not? He already has a sense that people ought not just do whatever comes to their minds. He is far from a Zen Master though. This Summer experience is important, but there's much to learn. He has already learned that to simply do what everyone else is doing is not necessarily right. So his childhood is not necessarily the father of his adulthood. He has certain characteristics, such as a thinking mind, and reflectiveness that will be a foundation to the rest of his life though.

Putting an ego-based approach to life. He can't quite make sure of what life is all about, but he knows it's not going well for him. He is concerned with his own confusion, pain, and the like. He is not yet in high school, and yet he has already started the journey. "Horrible, horrible disaster!" The Buddha would say about this. In addition, however the Buddha in his vast and endless compassion would say quietly and gently "almost everyone falls into the same trap my son." Our street musician soon to be Zen master is still in the delusion stage, but that's ok.

There we have it, the classical, typical start of yet another human life. Our street musician feels the angst, fear, humiliation, and anger that people just like him have been feeling at that stage of life for thousands of years. Perhaps more 20th or 21st century post-modern greed, self-centeredness, or apathy, but never-the-less through the vastly wise eyes of a Buddha it all is the same, the spinning of the wheel of life, and our street musician feels as if he is infinitely different. Of course he is different. He, regardless if he knows it or not is on the path to enlightenment, perhaps not in this life, but in years to come he will for the first time step into a Buddhist temple and be awed by what he sees. He will never turn back once he has entered the stream.

So all this feeling of differentness he feels is it real? Once when I attended a youth retreat at the City of Ten Thousand Buddhas the venerable master who was leading us encouraged us to ask ourselves "What is real?" Our future street musician asks himself, whither if he knows it or not "what is real? Who am I? What are all these crazy people doing to ME?" Yes, very similar; no identical to everyone else (well at least almost identical).

For our future street musician the strain, questions

242

of what to do, what can I, should I, would I, etc. etc. this is all very, very real. But this is good because regardless of his condition, he is thinking. This thinking, asking, wishing, and wondering will lead him to his spiritual path, his destiny. This dear reader is a good thing.

College

"No dude, no ... there is no way I would do that." The future street musician says. " I told you I have a girlfriend, I don't care how hot she is!" The street musician's college band had just finished a gig across the State. Mark, the drummer had found some nice local girls that were interested in fast moving musicians for an evening of fun. "Man, it's not like ... that I love Sarah ... you know? That is crazy. I mean to do something like that. I mean, do you like think it is a good idea or something?" Maybe asking if it were, a good idea was not exactly what our hero meant, but it was all he could think to say at the time. His friend and he had a moment or two of uneasy silence, then Mark started up again, trying to lighten the mood with a smile, " Come on dude! They are like so totally hot."

The future Zen master just looked down at the ground. They were at a stand-still. While he liked his friend, what the friend was suggesting was not in tune with who he was. The life of a free-spirited musician was fun, but sometimes it seemed as if the life, or at least the stereotype of the life was just not who he was.

The band had been doing gigs since his sophomore year. They were kind of famous almost, and traveling quite a bit. To a certain degree it hurt their studies. The future Zen master was a little uneasy about some aspects of the life of a road musician. He loved the music though, and it would see him through.

College too is a growing place. It is just a little more structured than the all encompassing "childhood." Here, in many cases one gets to be away from all those childhood friends, all those parents, all those people we knew for all those years. Here is a kind of re-birth, a chance to become someone new, and by this time we have experienced a bit of life so we have a slightly more clear idea of what exactly we want out of it. We step a little further into our life's path, and into what we call ourselves.

So what does college do to our street musician? Well, our street musician has been practising the guitar for a few many years now and really, really enjoys it and that is great. So he chooses to study music, that's great too. So where does this lead him? One major thing is that it will enable him to become the street musician which in many ways, along with his spiritual path, he was born to. Along with his musical studies he will take other courses that will help him in his future life. He will learn how to read and write better, do research, learn about economics, and history, and do algebra. He will continue to explore the who am I, who are you, what are you doing to me? questions. He will still for the most part put and I, I , I perspective on life taking the vantage point of an ego that wants, and needs, and must have, or must not have. Horrible, horrible says the Buddha. But that's life.

He learns music and its trade which are really great because it fills his heart with joy, makes him feel alive, makes him feel as if he can contribute something to this world, and make it a better place. He fills his mind with facts, and figures, and gains great skill on the keyboard and the fingerboard. He gets good grades, he is on the honour role.

So now he is a skilled musician, that's good, but it's only part of the picture. He is still looking for satisfaction, for something that will make him happy. He thinks he has found it because the music does touch something deep inside him, down to the roots of his being. But he is not enlightened yet. Still the pain of rejection from this girl or that hurts, still the ideas of "I'm better than you" haunt him, the egoism, arrogance, ignorance, pettiness, is still there. He has not yet stepped into that Buddhist temple. What a shame. But that is life to.

He graduates. He joins a rock band. They tour the country, then the world. He records many songs, he teaches at the local college after twenty years on the road and in the recording studio. He is not

 quite happy. Why?

He needs Zen.

Chapter II

The Entry of Zen

So you may ask does Zen alone make one happy? Of course not, that would be silly. However Zen does teach one to live as a whole human being. Zen is beyond happy or unhappy. And that is really, really, really, yes really great! Zen will teach our musician to live, to see reality for what it is, to be patient with his limited body and mind, to be wise, and to be free in the real sense.

Master Ji Ru of the Mid-American Buddhist Association once talked about how America is so free. But on the other hand, it, unlike some other countries does not really allow the freedom of the mind. Only the body is free for many Americans he said, with all the advertising and mass-consumer driven culture, and hype the mind is just spun around like a top. Zen is not really the jump up and down gleeful kind of happiness. Furthermore, it is not always about contentment, at least not in the day to day carrying out of our lives. It is release from all the negative stuff that keeps us from the path to enlightenment, a loss of all the negative behavior and ideas that bring us down. Like air conditioning is not the cooling of the air but the removal of the heat from it, so Zen is the removing of the negative. After that all the heat is gone, all we are left with is enlightenment, our Buddha nature.

So our friend is searching for something, things seem settled, but do they mean anything in the long term? He has a life, and it would seem a good one, but if all was well he wouldn't be searching around. He finds himself having genuine contempt for the audience, for the music, even for himself. Going from gig to gig he thinks, "these people don't have a clue what the music is about, they all rotten losers, this band stinks, what a jerk that drummer is, what am I doing here?" He plays lots of concerts but they don't mean anything because he just plays what sells, and the money is there in piles, it is just what sells. Cheap simple stuff, nothing really creative, nothing that he thinks is worthwhile.

Things go on like this for a while he doesn't really make any progress, until one night, after a concert he just goes straight home. No party, no signing autographs, no thank you, just thinking "hum, hum, what am I doing?" He shakes of his head and thinks "Why?"

He needs Zen.

The Teachings of Zen

What is this wonderful thing - this Zen - that our hero needs so badly? To be honest, (honesty with one's self and with others is at the heart of what Buddhism is) I can only tell you about Zen in my limited experience of it in 20th and 21st century USA, which may or may not be all that similar to centuries past in Japan where Zen, as adopted from the Chinese version of Buddhism developed. As I understand it, as I experienced at the San Francisco Zen Center, and at local groups throughout the USA, Zen is pretty much just straight Buddhism, with a slight twist of ancient Japanese cultural norms and values on occasion. Sometimes in modern American, some Caucasian hippyness is added in for good measure.

Zen embodies a strong mix of traditional Japanese culture, ethics, mentality, as well as Taoism (via Chinese Buddhism), and the old school orthodox Buddhist teachings. Zen in modern America is Buddhism first of all striped of ochre robes, golden pagodas and replaced with crispness, simpleness, dryness, black, symmetry, structure, and protocol; but mixed with American culture, or more often than not counter-culture of openness, friendliness, kindness, compassion, and freedom.

Zen has to a fairly large extent been "jazzed up" in the past few decades. Zen exists in the contemporary context in a slightly different strain than the real thing. Zen and the Art of Motorcycle Repair is just one example. People can even be caught saying "That's so Zen." What does it all mean? Japanese gardens, Fung Shui, etc. is all sort of in vouge. Regrettably though this process of coming in to the sphere of contemporary culture Zen and other things such at Fung Shui, Taoism, etc. have lost their meanings.

Zen emphasizes the sitting meditative practice of Buddhism. Given our street musician's unsettled feelings, a little quite sitting would do him some good. Zen means, in translation "to sit" and it was in a sitting position that the historical Buddha experienced enlightenment. That must be a good place to start then.

To revamp and re-teach fundamentals of Buddhism is pointless I think for my purposes. There are plenty of great books out there where a person can learn the basics, and not so basic teachings of Buddhism in all its flavours. Theravada, Zen, Mahayana,

Tibetan, etc. are all out there. However, for the sake of those who are new to Buddhism, I should at least offer a summary, especially pointed toward the direction this little tale leads. I would hope that not just those on the Buddhist path have picked up my book, perhaps just those impressed with the catchy title.

Buddhism basically teaches the relief of suffering. When pressed, this is what the Buddha would explain that this is the core of his teaching. Simple, to the point, with no claims to grandeur; the end of suffering in the world is what it is all about. He really made no other assurances other than that. He did not always say it brings enlightenment. Enlightenment, compassion, generosity, and wisdom all result but those are really not what the historical Buddha was after on his spiritual path. When he came to realize the transitory and dissatisfactory nature of life he struck out not so much to become "enlightened" as to end the cycle of constant births and deaths and earthy suffering. He, like most if not all Hindus seek relief from Samsara, the cycle of birth and death. The traditional context of Hinduism did not allow him to do what he needed to do. The cast system did nothing to lead him toward enlightenment so he left it. Caste means that one is to do the duties of one's station in life, ending the

251

cycle is not necessary a goal. In order to make his practice more direct he changed and adapted the practices he came in contact with. Whatever did not point directly and unquestionably to his goals he left. His belief in simplicity was important to his development, saying that in time, one on the path would lose all interest in rituals and ceremony. The food bowl, the robe, and practice are all he needed. That is best left to another discussion though. Buddhism and all its practices are rightly, in the Buddha's words aimed at the extinction of suffering, which means necessarily the extinction of birth of any kind; I would go so far as to say not even in the god realm. The historical Buddha told all sorts of tales about interaction with gods. There is little indication to say that they were enlightened. The foundations of Buddhism are the Four Nobel Truths, the Eightfold Nobel Path, non-self, Karma, and morality. I think it is enough to say that; you can go to countless monasteries, read books, or web sites to find the basics of Buddhism. My emphasis is on our street musician.

Our street musician finds himself totally burned out, disillusioned, aggravated, tired, and frustrated as many 21st century Americans do. "What is the point?" Some ask, "What does it all mean?" They ask in desperation. The noise and colors of the lunatic junk sellers at all the big corporations don't do it for us anymore. The gas guzzlers, big house in Orange County, perfect marital partner, holly wood nonsense entertainment, and 2.5 children don't do it either. What is going on? We need to go inside. The path as any true spiritual knower sees is inside. The Taoists of ancient China, the Zen masters, the Sufis of Islam, the Rabbis, priests, popes, Baptist preachers, Hindu Swamis, they all know, spiritual energy does not come from having toys, pleasing everyone around you, or material wealth. It comes through hard work. Internal work changing ourselves from the inside out. The path results in outer evidence of its self though. The halos of Christianity were adopted, according to Joseph Campbell from Buddhist images, the Buddha glowed to some, resulting in one asking him "What are you?" the response was "I am awake." An ease of the step, a soft glow of the heart and face, a gentleness with one's self and with the world around you. Coming from a knowing, a deep compassion, a mellowness, a sweetness, wisdom, as they sing at the City of Ten Thousand Buddhas in northern California "wisdom as vast as the sea."

Zen offers our street musician what he needs; but what is that exactly? The development from a delusional slob to enlightened being can be slightly different in each person. In fact it is, because each person has a different set of conditions, formations, ideas, environment, and personality traits. The basic lessons that are learned are fundamentally the same though. In the case of the street musician he does not seem to have any weird big ego trip to get over, no "I hate all you dirty slobs" entanglement, no "I am my body and it must be beautiful forever", no "I am my ideas and possessions" complex. So what is the main point of his hangup? It is that he is wondering what the point is of his life, what is the value of it, what can he give the world? This seems a pretty good place to be, relative to all the typical hangups that the Buddhist path slices through like a hot knife through butter.

He is already enlightened to the extent that many creative persons are. They are beyond the experience that is locked in just the head. They are beyond the seeing is believing state, and are at the level of consciousness that I believe the Buddha realized that knowing is believing, feeling in a deep way is believing. Seeing with the heart, spirit, gut, AND mind is believing. Knowing with the heart as well as the mind is the key to true belief. Part of Zen is the use and study of Koans - short stories, questions, or anecdotes which are often nonsensical at first glance but in hindsight can be amazing and profound. The question of "what is Zen?" can be asked and answered as a Koan such as "The only true answer is the one you find for yourself." It dodges the question but at the same time gives it the only true and honest answer there can be. A classic Koan is "What is the sound of one hand clapping?" Can there really be an answer to this?

Logic is completely irrelevant in Zen. In some traditions; the forest tradition of Thai Buddhism for example does emphasis scholarly knowledge and logic to understand the Buddha's teaching, and this is fine, but I think it stand in stark contrast to asking "What is the sound of one hand clapping?" This sort of shock to the mind is what is meant to be achieved in Zen, at least in some times, it makes you "awaken" in a very visceral, bodily sort of way. In the Renzai tradition of Zen (and others) hitting a person during meditation was a technique used that supposedly would enlighten a person in a second. Asking Koans helps a person to get off their high-horse of scholarly monasticism, and out of the rut of day-to-day thinking. When confronted with such a seemingly nonsensical thing, I think one cannot help but just stop and smile. If you get it, surely you must be on the right path. It makes sense to someone who has done a lot of meditation because you realize that all the ego created type of thinking, all the labelling, judging, comparing, trying to understand and compartmentalize will not help. Just being there in the moment to say "I haven't the foggiest idea what he is talking about" shows you that you understand at least a bit about the Buddhist, and in particular the Zen mind. The empty mind is something emphasized also in Zen, unlike other traditions. There is nothing that empties my mind as well as being confronted like something like "what is the sound of one hand clapping?" and then just chuckling, and thinking "I've got it." That can be the greatest feeling in the world, just that.

So a musician does very much empty his mind on the stage. Often a musician will not really be able to account for every moment on stage. In the same way meditators can sit for 40 minutes and feel as if it were just 2. The music absorbs him completely. He is just there in the moment as a meditator is, living that moment completely. Not wanting to go to the party afterward, not wanting to argue with the stage manager, or his lawyer, or his wife, but simply doing the work that must be done, savouring it, absorbing it, being in it, and around it, and through it. The meditator is not waiting for a lunch break, not waiting until the bell rings, or until the dog scratches the door; he is there fully and completely, doing the work of the meditator, feeling the cushion under him, the breath going in and out, watching feelings, thoughts, emotions as they bubble out of his mind. He is fully completely, and richly there, so is Eric Clapton when he plays, so was Jascha Heifitz, or any other of the greats. At times they do "come out of it" (or maybe I should say go into it) bring their awareness into the things around them, that is tune into the drummer's solo, or pick up on the vibe from the audience, but in many ways this is a subconscious thing they must do anyway to play with the others. When a musician is starting, he must carefully pay attention to the other players, must count, and think, "second finger third fret, two beats" and the like in order to do what a musician does, but he is just a beginner at that point. He has not found the Zen of the music, he has not really "become one" with it the way the greats have. So really Zen teaches us just to be human. To be in the moment(s) (yes I have to admit there are many moments in a human life) of life as a human. Buddha nature and enlightenment is as natural to the human as playing is to the musician. It defines us, because strictly speaking in some traditions only in a human life can one be enlightened, a human life is the point of human life, it is the last stop, the destination, the key, the only condition in which body and intellect combine in such a way as to enable our minds to enter into the understanding we need to attain the goal. Any artist, such as a sculptor, painter, writer, or musician becomes absorbed into his/her work in such a way as to realize a certain amount of selflessness that is required for enlightenment in the Buddhist meaning, a freedom from volitions (other than the one at hand), attachments (other than the artist's goal), and desires (other than again the goals of the artist) are present. So really artists understand a bit of what Buddhism teaches, but still there is attachment to the material world. In fact their world is all about sensation, and this is unfortunately a great hindrance to enlightenment.

Non-attachment is a great foundation of Zen and Buddhism in general. The wishes, desires, and volitions that come with attachment lead us to be born again according to Buddhist teaching. We cannot be free if we are filled with all sorts of worldly goals, like eating cherry pie, playing Mozart, or finding a girlfriend. They are incredible distractions to the Zen practitioner. If we dream of having that last piece of cherry pie just as we die surely we will be born as a bakers daughter. Right? The Zen mind is free from those things, empty, clean, pure, free from wishes, or any volution to do, or say, or be.

So, our hero knows what it is to truly be in the moment, but still has attachment to his art, and a little delusion as well. Being in the moment is a great asset though, and has felt that incredible relief that comes as a result, even though he needs a little work before becoming a Zen master. In the Devata-samutta, from the Theravada scriptures 1.10 "The Wilderness" the Buddha was engaged in discussion with a devata asking him how the monks could endure such a harsh existence, the response of the Buddha was "They don't sorrow over the past, don't long for the future. They survive on the present. That's why their faces are bright and serene. From longing for the future, from sorrowing over the past, fools wither away like a green reed cut down." Our character is not enduring any great physical hardships like a wilderness, but he does know the joy of just being present in the moment. It takes an amazing amount of presentness to be a performer as he is. He is absorbed into the music, he IS the music. I recall some of the video recordings of Herbert von Karajan the famous Austrian conductor. He was so absorbed into the music he seemed to become it. Totally taken in, is poured forth from every pore, every motion, every intention. Karajan WAS the music, when on stage, he became the Beethoven Fifth Symphony, or whatever was being played at the time.

This artist, our street musician like many others sees that life is more than what meets the eye. That the stuff going on inside the body as effected by the mind is so important. Life is not about ideas, or things, it is about experience. It is not all logical either, this experience of life. Being there on stage feeling the rush of the energy from thousands of excited fans can not be explained, only felt deep down in one's being. As Oliver Wendell Holmes said "the life of the law is not in logic, but in experience." The same is the case for Buddhist practice, and musical practice. It must be played live in order for it to make any sense. On the page, or stuck in a philosophical discussion it does no good. Music is only music once it is played. It is so subtle in some ways; you can not bottle it, or frame it, or really necessarily explain it. Only the experience can make it what it is. Likewise the life of our musician and the training of Zen is
one of experience. Feeling out every second and millisecond, examining it, making sense of it in the context of all the other milliseconds we have experienced through out our lives.

Zen means to sit. Not to sit and rest, but sit and open up our minds to every thought, sensation, and mental experience. In a Zendo, a Zen meditation hall everything is prepared for this process of sitting and experiencing. For me sometimes it is like sitting in a jet or a race car. The amazing sensation of all the crazy ideas, feelings, emotions, and mental pictures as they go either whizzing by, or stand their and wait for my attention either pulling me forward or making me jump back in repulsion. I've have never gone so far with out really going physically somewhere than when I am on the meditation cushion. It is amazing.

However, Zen sitting does not necessarily mean that we will hear the buzzers, or get any kind of massive insight, or feel like a jet fighter rushing through mental experiences, some times we just sit there and experience the breath, the in-out of it, the heaviness of the body, and the unbearable boredom of it all. But we do our time, we re-enforce our spiritual path, we step, regardless if we realize it that moment closer to the goal. Jack Kornfield, one of the greatest lay Buddhist teachers of our time describes it as "going no where, being on one." At that point we simply be, which is the key to the Buddha's practice.

Chapter III

Zen and Artists, Zen and This Artist

Zen is the art of living. Of all the sects of Buddhism known today, I believe Zen is the most compatible to art and artists. Zen paintings and sculptures are fairly well known: Bodhidharma with his eyelid free eyes, the circle drawn with Japanese calligraphy brush, or the fat frog. The design of Zen structures, as well as the placement of things in those structures are very artistically done. An artist's eye is needed to do it. As with all traditional Japanese culture the design, format, and presentation of things are very important to Zen. Beauty is extremely important in Zen, regardless if people go around saying "The Zendo must look beautiful." it DOES have to be beautiful in one way or the other.

Zen is a religion, or a sect of a religion, but Zen is also life. Zen, as its predecessor in China, Ch'an is a mix of Taoism and Buddhism, or Buddhism as related and understood in Taoist terms. I believe Buddhism as understood by Taoist can not help but be a hybridization. The Taoists, and also Confucianists of ancient China both were extremely artistic. Painting, poetry, tea ceremony, all went hand in hand with their practices of meditation, philosophizing, and living a simple life. They understood art in a very intimate way because their lives were more or less art forms, beautiful sculptures carved out of life its self. Complete with form and finish, glowing in a soft light and standing the test of time, just as well or better than any by the ancient Greeks or Romans.

This all transferred with Ch'an to Japan, but of course they had their own artistic way of life before Zen. Long before Zen arrived in Japan there were wonderful tea gardens, Shinto temples, pomp, circumstance, Geisha, and Samurai. All this certainly evokes a sort of artistic sensibility that is refined and subtle, and truly magnificent. The Taoists such as Lu Tzu and others were contemplating poetically and writing poems of tea right along the new alien religion (Buddhism) and all this accumulated before the Japanese learned of it. This artistic sentiment is "teaism" as was written of in the Book of Tea by Kakuzo Okakura. This book while not really standard Zen literature adds a great deal to the subject, and allows those new to Zen, but not new to fine living or art some insight in to Zen. The author writes in a way somewhat unfamiliar with Zen, I would not mistake him for a Zen master anymore than the everyday Japanese, but his sentiments, regardless if he knows or not are classic Japanese, and classic Zen. Other artistic predecessors of Zen are the Taoist writings of Yang Chu in his Garden of Pleasures writing (in my paraphrase) "To deprive the ear is to not give it beautiful music, to deprive the eye is to not give it beautiful sights." He emphasizes the use and enjoyment of art for the sake of a full and spiritual life. Zen goes well with art, and as it happens to be artists as well, not to mention our artist.

The problem our musician senses is that there is no real meaning in what he does. He has professional fortune, but of course as a true artist he feels there is more to life than a job well done. He's not just doing what he does to make millions like they do in Hollywood, nor is he trying to sell some imaginary image of himself. He is the real thing, a real musician: a Muddy Waters, or Beethoven, or Eric Clapton. He is playing well, and even living well, but does not see the importance or impact of what he is doing. Maybe he shouldn't. This is where the Zen and the Street Musician come in. Up to now there has only been a musician who has had some experience with Buddhism. So now he has been meditating. What has he learned? That he can't sit still very easily. That his body hurts and his mind spins around like a top, jumping from this thought to that, from this emotion to that. It never settles, it never sees the Buddha-ness of life its self, but through it all he is changing, he is becoming what he is at his fundamental state. The fact that he is drained and felt unfulfilled after a concert means that he is already in a way taped into his Buddha nature.

So, he goes on to experience yet another type of Buddhism, Zen. He visits his local Zen Center. The people are nice, the building immaculately clean, the walls plain and eggshell white, the black robes and cushions impressive, "nice" he thinks to himself. After a while he sees that really Zen and the older Theravada school that he was introduced to are pretty much the same.

He continues to practice Zen for about five years, and continues his musical career as well, playing concerts, teaching, etc. Life is good. All those Zen teachings are a little difficult to get his head around at times, and further even more difficult to have make any sense in the context of his life, but he's getting there.

For me, Zen is particularly applicable to musicians, because in some ways Zen is devoid of the scholarly structure of other Buddhist schools, but is filled with ceremony and protocol. Artists both like and dislike both these things in the same order as Zen. The timing of when to or not do something on stage, when to do a curtain call, where to place a piece of art or not place it, is all very important in context. Yet strict protocol, for the sake of doing things a certain way grates on music. Structure can destroy a jazz session, or a composition in any form, but it also can make some sense of the raw material that art is made of.

Our musician, soon to be street musician has a lot to think about, and so do we, so let's think a little about what exactly art and Zen have to offer each other.

A Sense of Purpose

Life for artists and Zen practitioners is an urgent matter, and not to be taken lightly. Artists know not to waste their lives. One of the greatest teachings of Zen is to not waste one's life. I remember being almost horrified at the eery sound of the hammer hitting the han in the mornings I stayed at the San Francisco Zen Center. According to Zen the han is used to remind us of the transitory nature of our life. The han is a wooden board that is hit to call people to meditation, and also mark the times of day, such as the midday meal. Over time the han becomes worn thinner and thinner, eventually, like our bodies becoming worn out. Often it bears some poetry along the lines of "don't waste your life." It is hit in a sort of slow timed pattern and then allowed to bounce quickly in drum roll fashion. Bounce, bounce, bounce, bbbbbbounce as the hitter holds her arm still allowing the hammer to reflect off the surface on its own, according to its own weight, and her grip strength in perfect harmony, in the frequency that is the perfect balance of the hitter, the hammer, and the board, in a completely organic way. In a way that is one hundred percent Zen. So it is struck to remind us to come do our morning meditation, not waste our life, as the board is slowly used up, much in the way our hours of life in our present body are used up.

Art and artists as Zen and Zen practitioners deal with important and real stuff. The stuff that is at the end of the day the most important stuff there is to do. There is no time for MTV, or silly sitcoms, or wasteful gossip. Life with all its urgency and importance is going on now, it is the main event, it is the most important order of the day. Through time in the studio, on stage, in the Zendo people transform themselves in very real ways, they are so engaged in life that they are able to notice the subtle, and sometimes not so subtle changes to their psyches, and "selves". It is basically introverted stuff being an artists or Zen master so one can not help but get to know one's self. Artists' style changes in dramatic ways over time, at least if they are actively engaged in creating art rather than a mass produced product to get rich at. Likewise for Zen practitioners. I remember thinking back to ideas I had years ago, reading my journals sometimes, and it is amazing how different I was "back then." Even more amazing is how we sometimes go back to some positions we had, and then abandoned, but then go back to but in a new and renovated way. The founder of the London Buddhist Society - Christmas Humphreys - entitled his autobiography Both Sides of The Circle and in many cases this is what happens to Zen practitioners. Really you are never far from home in the spiritual sense. The Buddha sought enlightenment not in some distant land, or in some weird meditation-enhanced Jhana state (There are four main Jhana states in meditation, they describe the experience and mind state; usually come in succession as the mind becomes more calm and "absorbed" into the experience. They are also called "absorptions") but right here, right now. This is one of the most valuable teachings of Zen, the Zen mind. The Zen mind is pretty much the everyday mind. The mind that decides how much salt to put in the broth, or which slab to lay for the stairway, or which book to pick for a research project, or which road to take are all very much the Zen mind. Just being in the moment, doing what's required, nothing more. No need to complicate things, no need to create castles and cathedrals of delusion in our minds, just BE. Be in the moment, be there to enjoy the mystery of life, that's the way to do it.

Artists and Zen masters live for the greater good. They know that they are connected to something great. In the case of the Zen master the connection is with thousands of years of Buddhist practice. They practice in that lineage, and it really is powerful stuff when you think about it. The historical Buddha really put his neck out when he announced to his family he knew already he would be enlightened and never born again, it took strength to do what he felt he must do and seek a spiritual path outside his palace. He helped the world in teaching it the most refined, condensed, and masterful spiritual practice there is. That is true kindness, true greatness. Best of all it is really simplicity in its self. The Buddhist merely calls reality for what it is. She does not get lost in the ego struggles, the grasping for this and that, once that is done there really can be no re-birth because the ego does not seek any thing more. It does not want to knock Johnny down a peg or two, does not want that last slice of chocolate cake, does not want to get that last ten million dollars, or take that last trip to Paris. With this new found insight the Buddhist naturally seeks to make life better for the whole of humanity. Likewise the artists in some ways sees through the smoke and mirrors of life. Over the St. Louis Art Museum it states "Art Still Has Truth. Seek It There." Nothing could be more for the greater good than giving the world truth.

Art is true because it springs from the human spirit, nothing but a human, (at least that we know of so far, other solar systems may prove this wrong) can create art. It springs from a sense of connectedness, of goodness, of life, and happiness, and freedom. I think any true artist would have to agree with that. When creating she or he feels an almost undescribable joy and wholeness. They give the most amazing gift to the world when they create their art. Truly it is a creation they alone can give, it is beautiful and adds value and meaning to the peoples' lives who behold it. This is the greater good - making the world a better place. A more beautiful world, a more meaningful world, a kinder world, a more colourful world. Amazing.

Buddhism takes guts, it cuts against things that society would offer up as the do all and end all. Its heroic in a way. Giving of yourself for others is truly the highest of callings. I remember when I worked for the Washington Public Interest Research Group, one of the State "Pirgs" as they are called. Each US State has one to the best of my knowledge. They are the ones who come knocking on your door and tell you to vote to save the National Forests from the Republicans and similar things. Every day we started out by saying "Welcome to a new day in the fight for the public interest, where we fight the good fight and we fight to win." We did not just say it, we screamed it. It was done with a little humour to be honest, but in retrospect those are really strong and courageous words when you think about it. I think that the Buddha and Zen masters could say the same thing when they begin a new day.

Buddhists are truly courageous. It is not a simple matter to come to terms with some of the most important, and often unpleasant aspects of human life; to accept the reality that we are not always who we think we are, who we would like to be, or that we have done horrible things. In a way they are warriors, brave and right people, like the Samurai. It takes courage to let go of all those things that we think are so important, to think outside of our narrow senses of reality. I will never forget when Matt Flickstein, a young budding Buddhist teacher who trained in part at the Bhavana Society in West Virginia said "People don't really love the people they say they do." He explained that in most cases a person's "love" for another is based on static conditions, or what the person gets out of the relationship. Once those things change the whole relationship ends, because it is only a conditional "love" we have for the people. True love is more than what people say they have on a daily basis. I think in a way he was even questioning the idea of love. It does make sense. In almost all situations the "love" people have is just attachment so something, or neediness. People want this or that out of a relationship and when they don't get it all bets are off. They want someone to "love" them, or give then an ego boost, or hold their hand, or do their laundry, or look beautiful; when the other person no longer is or does whatever the person wants the relationship dissolves A mother's love comes closest to real love, I think. Still then I think it could be understood as just a mother's want to fill their biological urge to care for their offspring. That is the sort of thing that really gives a person a kick in the pants, that really motivates, stirs, and shakes up the Buddhist. To face the wall of delusion, the vice-grip of the ego, and slice through it. A great Zen teacher of mine who worked as a lawyer negotiating contracts for a city government used a Tibetan image to motivate herself. The figure is shown with a sword raised high above her head about to smash a skull, which can represent delusion, or death, or really the death that delusion causes. Before meeting people she would go into the rest room and assume the pose of the Tibetan goddess. She said it was amazing. It is not the sort of crazed lashing out at what hurts us that our ego makes us do, but the skilled and mindful cutting of a Samurai or the mental cutting a Zen master uses on his ego. The artist and the Zen master offer this greatness to the world.

Go to any outdoor music festival and just feel the energy given off my both players and listeners. It does not really matter what the genre is, folk, pop, country, R&B, etc. It's amazing isn't it? Both players and listeners feel as if they are part of something more important in some ways than that on which life depends. It is more important than food, or drink or shelter. The creation and enjoyment of their life fills them with such joy, solace, sense of comfort, that in a way that space they are in as they play or enjoy the playing is all that really exists. They feel they are part of something important and real, something urgent. Much the same for the Zen meditation master. While she or he is there in that moment of whatever it is - pain, joy, insight, boredom, etc. that is really all that exists, it is in a way WHO that person is, embodying his/her being at that point. Does that make sense? In other words the meditator is absorbed into the thought or sensation in a way so that she IS that thought or sensation just as an artist in a way BECOMES the piece of music or art work she is creating. In Zen of course a person is not suppose to dwell on the sensations, or thoughts, but merely let them pass through her existence, however I have found that in doing so while one does not attach to the thought or sensation one is really there with it, not pushing it away and not grasping for it. They say "if you hit a Zen master will he scream? Of course because in fact it really hurts a great deal to be hit." The master is simply being there in the moment to experience fully what there is to experience. In the same ways musicians really enjoy playing because they are really there to experience it, with their whole bodies. All the joys and sorrows are felt truly, deeply, and fully, with heart, and mind, and soul.

Artists do what they do because it makes them feel whole. The same is true for Zen masters. There is no greater sense of being grounded, of doing right, or coming home that experiencing an extended retreat of Buddhist practice. It is through these that one can truly become in a way a child again, but also mature into a rich and full human being. We lose all the weird ego-based stuff that society puts on us, all the sadistic demands, all that would have us transform ourselves into people we truly are not, all the self-destroying ideas, and moods, and goals. We become children again, in a sense, but also become very wise children. We are childish like any artist is. They just play really, play with sound, or wood, or plaster, or paint. They play because it is who they are, and to do anything differently would separate them from who they are. It would ask be asking them to break themselves to do that. Children are moody though aren't they? They have tantrums. So does almost every Hollywood actor, every rock musician, every painter. Emotions are part of the human bargain; however not part of the Zen bargain. We'll get to that later.

Artists and Zen masters live for the greater good. They live a life with meaning, and fulfilment. They live not so much for greedy desires but they life how they do because it connects them with who they are deep down. In fact it would be impossible for them to live any other way. They live connected to life, and to all people everywhere. They understand the mutual aspects of human life, that we all are in this thing together. They live to create something beautiful, something real, something human in every sense of the word. They are not concerned with the petty "me, me, me" "I, I, I," of the mass majority of people, they understand the gifts they have, and that those gifts must be shared.

Likewise for our hero, he lives for the greater good. He, from the very beginning of his life knew he should make something of it. While the first few years were somewhat unclear for him, as time went on he knew he should be someone more than just the next guy down the street. Life is important to him, but the meaning of life has to a certain extent evaded him. He feels lost, and is looking for what he lacks. He is looking for his sense of purpose, and it will take a few years of maturity and growth for this to happen.

He does his gigs, and by the age of twenty-five he has a grasp of his profession, but he does not have a grasp of life. He has travelled throughout the United States. He has played for large crowds and small. He has played country fairs, college festivals, and the like. He has had fun, and made a substantial amount of money, but as he matures he comes to realize it is empty of real meaning. He must look deeper to see what life should mean. The foundations of his introspection were laid in childhood, but his true spiritual destination is still a bit further down the path.

Life is urgent for both artist and Zen master. Life is not to be wasted. Artists and Zen masters are exceptionally special people. It is urgent to become enlightened, to learn as much as possible in order to avoid a negative re-birth. To avoid evil at all cost. It is urgent to create what you were born to create, to beautify the world, to create joy, to avoid evil, to make the world what it must be by your existing. Urgent to create a beautiful, whole, special, full, unique life.

Artists know there is more to life than amassing wealth, eating fine food, doing drugs, or having a nice car. Even though many do get involved in these activities. Some thing as brought them to be artists other than those things - at least if they are great. They are doing it because if is in their very beings. A great blues man, one of the old timers in the early days of recording, I believe Johnny Johnson said "the blues was in me and it had to get out." John Lee Hooker said similar things. It is a great loss if a great genius does not allow the world to take part in that magical wonder of his or her talent. In addition, the artist does not fully come to be what he or she truly is, because that sort of talent is not by accident. Buddhism teaches there are no accidents. People make mistakes for sure, but no cosmic accidents.

The venerable Hua who founded the City of Ten Thousand Buddhas in Ukiah California was on a trip with a young monk. On arrival at the Los Angles airport the young monk noticed how horrible people were behaving and said "oh master how horrible these people really need to hear the Dharma." That may be true on one level, but the master responded by saying "everything is exactly the say it should be." Everything makes sense from the Zen perspective, because everything IS, and there is no other possible way for it to be.

This sense of purpose that Zen and art brings is an amazingly satisfying thing. It allows one to feel at home with ones self. So much of society is all about feeling inadequate, I think that is a real disaster we have created for our selves in the past fifty years or so. Not that people did not have ambition earlier, ambition is not really what I am talking about. Napoleon had ambition, J D Morgan, and the Buddha himself in a subtle, gentle, but amazingly strong way all had ambition. It is the feeling of "I must, I must, I must or I won't be good enough." That is increasingly pushed on us, the marketers, and the super models, and the salespeople. Its all crazy to the musician and the Zen practitioner. They feel at home in any situation, because they are grounded, they know who they are, and they know what the world is. They feel no need to be someone they are not, to create some persona that the advertising industry has created for them because they are so much greater than that.

The purpose of life for Zen Master and artist is to create a masterpiece of life. A wonderful, unique, special, powerful, full, human, and perfect human life. There is in a sense no time for games, but in fact they whole thing in a way is a game. As Shakespear said "The whole world's a stage and every man a player." Both artist and Zen master know that life is to be taken seriously, but not TOO seriously that we miss the point. The point being that all those dramatic things our egos create for us are just smoke and mirrors in a magician's bag of tricks. That really in the end most of the ego trips, and "I must do, or have, or not do" is all a bunch of nonsense that distracts us from the real game at hand - the "game" as it were of becoming enlightened or becoming who we really are. Both realize it is a fine balance of strident effort, and a relaxed approach. We must be able to laugh at ourselves if we are to make progress toward our
goals of masterpieces of life.

I cannot say that artists are meant to be in a sort of

cosmic sense. That the world would have ended if Beethoven, or Mahler, or U2, or the Beatles had not existed, but the circumstances that allow artists to be artists are great and powerful stuff. There are plenty of bands and players that would like to be making money out there, but those blessed with the right combination of talent, opportunity, and circumstances are in a way "born" to become what they are. There is no other possible way for them to live, as according to venerable Courtin of the Tibetan Buddhist tradition teaches, once a person has set a certain karmic circumstance in place at the time of death there is no possible way for them to be born in any other way than what those circumstances dictate. Example; a fisherman, someone who has a strong fascination with fishing, catching fish, eating fish etc, there is some thing in the previous life or lives that have accumulated so that there is no possible way he or she could have done anything else. The karmic desires, ideas, and facinations with fish have destined this person to be born a fisherman in the next life. So while the world does not NEED artists, the people that are to be born to become artists have made their own destiny through their karmic good deeds, and desires.

The Artistic Sentiment

281

What exactly is the artistic sentiment? You may ask. Art is about the use of the senses, about creating something that appeals to the senses , and tells a story of sorts, or makes a statement. Art is made to be appreciated for how it affects the mind in combination with the body. Buddhism also uses this mind/body combination but in many ways the goals are completely opposite of those in art. In Buddhism one is to use the body/mind to realize the conditioned and transitory nature of our existence. In art one is to engage the joy of the body/mind enjoying all the sensual experiences one can have. Michael Tilson Thomas, the conductor of the San Francisco Symphony explained that everyone thinks classical music is all about the intellect, but nothing could be farther from the truth. It is a physical, and guttural experience. A short listen to any Mahler, Tchaikovsky, or Korngold will prove this. Art is sensual indulgence, Zen in some ways is the escape from the senses.

Art is about creating something, being something, expressing one's self. So you ask isn't this the exact opposite of what our street musician will accomplish in Zen? In a word "yes". This is what the street musician is struggling with. However, let's not get the cart before the horse. So he decides one day, just by chance to do something he has never done before, walk into a Buddhist temple. Why? Since childhood he was in fact involved in Karate, Tai Kuan Do, and other Asiatic activities later, in college he took one of those world religion courses the colleges make people take these days. No little surprise, Buddhism and all its derivations were included. At the time he thought it was nice, but it did not really make a huge impression on him. It would be a while yet after his first exposure to Buddhism that its full effect would be felt. You see Zen, and all Buddhism is about the sowing of seeds, not literal seeds, at least not all the time, but seeds of ideas that set our future direction. They are Karmic seeds, sown either not long ago, or eons ago. It can be very subtle. A glance from someone here, or a brief read of a phrase there, but as our behaviour dictates our karma for future lives, so in the present life our experiences can affect who we become in the short term. So, impressed by the golden gables of his local Thai temple he goes in, and is completely amazed and overpowered by what he experiences. Why you ask? A bunch of shaven headed little men sitting on the floor with sheets wrapped around them? That I think is also karma. A combination of things, a ripening, the fruition of things I mentioned at the beginning, all come to play in our lives. Here a combination of past lives and activities in this life have proven to drive our hero into a Buddhist temple for solace. I think that's a good thing.

He sits in the total and absolute silence and is awestruck by how wonderfully gentle the little men in orange robes are, how serene, shiny, beautiful. The smell of incense, bitter, pungent, filling the air as it glides slowly up and out across the faces of the golden Buddha statues, as he sits in awe. It makes an impression on him. One that will not pass away ever.

Art and Zen are about both style and substance. "The clothes make the man." In fact one is interlocked in such a way with the other that they are inseparable - style and substance that is. The way things are done in Zen has everything to do with the technique of the path, there is a reason why things are strict - discipline of body leads to discipline of mind. The controlled actions in what seems a silly ceremony lead to a quieting of the mind and understanding of the teachings.

The style, form, and structure of an artistic work both makes it and defines it. The fast tempo and repeated themes of a classical music rondo both make it what it is, and allow you to put a label on it. Take a guitar solo by any of the famous players, their style shows you that it is them, and also makes the style what it is. The components add that special character to it, allow it to be what it is, and allow you to recognize it as say Jimmy Hendrix in year X, or BB King, or Sting, or anybody. Style can of course just make something pretty, but it also gives you something to sink you teeth into.

As with Zendos and also the Shaker buildings in North America, the cleanness of lines, the plain white walls and the simpleness of the furniture and furnishings all allow the practice of the religion to function as it should, but also give the more simple features of our human nature something to interact with, to recognize, and be home with. They in their pure simpleness, allow the simplest, but also most complex of human nature, the Buddha nature to come out. By setting the scene so to speak, with an overwhelming direct and simple artistic design the setting brings out these things in the practitioners. These qualities design, define, create and MAKE the Zendo and the Shaker building what they are. The style is substantial in that it helps guide and shape the spiritual practice.

So what does the artistry of Zen have to do with our future street musician? Being an artist, he naturally has an artistic sentiment. Zen has a substantial artistic sentiment which he will absorb more and more fully as time goes on. Just as Zen is made by its clothes, using the "Clothes make the man" idea, our musician can appreciate the depth of Zen through its artistic clothing. He spends more and more time practicing meditation, first at the Theravada temples,

Zen as Opposed to the Artistic Sentiment

You are probably wondering at this point dear reader "Where in the world is the street musician." This junction is where the street musician comes into being. Where the musician becomes a street musician. Our musician has learned a good deal of Buddhist teachings, has embodied them, and accepted them wholly. He feels a bit off though, a bit uncomfortable with his life, with who he is, he is trying to make sense of it all. This is the rub. It is at the junction where Zen becomes opposed to art that the musician becomes a street musician, and he comes to realize that it is time for change.

Art is for the most part about appealing to the senses, while Zen is about enlightenment. The Lotus Sutra's "no eyes, no body, no mind, no etc. no etc." Drives home the point that Buddhism is in part about getting to know no-self. That is the teaching of how we are limited, in the long-term we don't really exist, at least in the way we think we do (or some of us think we do). To a certain necessary degree art and Zen cannot co-exist. The historical Buddha said "I teach the ending of suffering." The Dalai Lama said "What I teach is kindness." These do summarize the teachings of Buddhism, but at the heart of it, it is about destroying the ego and delusion. Art often relies on a bit of delusion to be what it is. It is not really real unless we think it is real. Beauty is in the eye of the beholder. The experience that art creates relies on our buying into the story it is selling. The facts do not stare you in the face the way the Buddhist teachings of no-self, or the fact of suffering can stare you in the face; solid, unmoving, unending, and uncompromising. In order to believe the truths, say any typical rock band is selling these days, or many of the past generation a person must buy into the way they see the world. The hippies protesting Vietnam for example, yes war is bad, killing is bad, but is all the sex and pot (marijuana) smoke really necessary, all the hating your parents, and the US Government just for the sake of it? That sort of truth does not make a whole lot of sense. Many artists present things that are very conditioned by transitory things - such as emotions. Emotions are real in one sense, but in another sense they are just invented because of our out look on things. Me dropping my ice cream cone may make me cry, but you may laugh. The emotions are real, but not in an everlasting sense that the major world religions teach.

The Four Noble Truths have been true ever sense there have been human beings, Van Gogh's truths I cannot be so sure about. Some art is universal and everlasting: The loneliness depicted in "Alice's World", isolation of the post-modern world in "Night Hawks", or the horrors of the Spanish Civil War pictured by Picasso. The door of fate knocking in Beethoven's Fifth Symphony I'm not so sure about; Buddhism teaches that we make our own fate, we choose the Karmic actions that create our future.

The fact of the matter is that one simply cannot live a double life, this is the truth of Zen and of true art. One must be wholly, fully, and completely with one's self without counter dictions. Zen, unfortunately is not completely one with the temper tantrums of Hollywood actors, the sexual antics of rock stars, or any other of the negative behaviours of artists today. While Zen-life is beautiful as any Picasso or Monet is, it does cut down the emotional ups and downs that lead artists to live - in many ways "an artist's life." Artist believe they need their

288

emotional drama to create art, maybe they do, because art is emotional and getting in touch with it does enable one to picture it on canvas or out of sound waves. For the artist the emotions and the depiction of the emotions are real, for the Zen master the emotions are just a passing mirage in the desert. Our simple minds cook them up, make them real because they strike so strongly on our organism.

Unfortunately so much of art is based on silly emotional stuff, especially after the 19th century when romanticism took over 18th century enlightenment. The enlightened leaders in the new world such as Jefferson and Franklin were deists who believe in the use of the rational mind and science to better man's plight. The romanticists who followed in the next century believed man is an emotional being (and rightly so) and as such the used and enjoyment of the emotions is not a bad thing. However it does lead to delusion, especially in the Buddhist sense. Jefferson and Franklin thought that the leaders of the nation should be educated and wise people, and of course from this we get the US Constitution the best written constitution in world history. Romantic artists such as Edgar Allen Poe, Beethoven, Schubert, Mahler, Bizet, and Charles Dickens all embody this sort of reckless enjoyment of emotion. Dealing with ghosts, goblins, the hand

of fate
knocking, witch hunts, and Jewish emotional angst.
This is not really the place to discuss how
emotionalism and romanticism changed the art
world and in fact society, at least in the West
dramatically; however I do think I should explain a
little though. The 18th century was one of
modernization of ideas, the discovery of science, and
the use of form, and skill, democratization, and
knowledge to better man's plight. The growth of
deism as practised by Thomas Jefferson and
Benjamin Franklin in the New World is a clear
example of how the enlightenment worked. They
simply could not come to terms and advocate a
formal religious practice when it simply made no
sense to do so. Likewise, the true artist does not go
into emotional fits just for grins, he does so because
the art tells him to, because it demands it.

So it is here, we find our hero. At the age of thirty
he is an able musician, but not an able person. He
loves the roar of the crowd, the fans, the publicity,
he loves the good it brings him, but as time goes on
he loses himself for the music. No longer does he
play the music, but it plays him. He needs the music
to live, but paradoxically, it is sucking the life from
him, because it is time for him to progress spiritually.

He begins to live a double life of sorts. It is an imbalance that buts him off balance as he learns more and more about the true meaning of life. He likes the music, but the superficiality of it becomes clearer and clearer. He feels lost like a man out at sea. The sea of his experience washes him to and fro. He has lost his sense of identity, and only through challenging it can he make his way home. It has become too much of a do whatever feels good mentality for him, he realizes the importance of substance, and not just doing what feels good.

Likewise in Zen. There is no "feel good" mentality in Zen, no feeding off the emotions, no playing around for the sake of play. In my personal opinion Buddhism is the most streamlined, down-to-earth, to-the-point, sensible, and practical religions on earth. In comparison other religions lead one down strange and dark paths of superstition, stupidity, useless ritual, and over simplification. The historical Buddha said "What I teach is the end of suffering." And really nothing more needs to be said as far as an explanation of it. Buddhists don't take part in the "feel good", or in many cases the feel "bad" emotionalism encouraged in other religions, and especially in the art world. Everything points to the path to enlightenment, nothing is done to appeal to the emotions, to trick the followers into believing, or

for the sake of show. Every practice, teaching, and discourse leads clearly and unstoppably toward the goal. Art is so much
about getting into the feeling of things, of enjoying, or hating the human emotional experience. For the Buddha all this was to be understood, not to waste any time with. I think likewise is the case of Buddhism's stance on God or gods. The historical Buddha talked with them, taught them, knew of them. People claim that Buddhism is an atheistic religion, this is not really true. He never denied the gods, in fact the Theravada texts are filled with references to them. What he did say was that "Verily I say to you that there are too many religions claiming that worship of a god will lead to a birth in a heaven realm." I think similarly it could be said that there are too many people that make too much of the emotions. Being lead by them invariably toward disaster.

Art is about the ego and about egotistical motives; Buddhism is not. The Buddha taught of the release of the stranglehold of the ego, about forgetting all that silly stuff that people everyday torture themselves with. The goals of beautifying the body, accumulating Mercedes, accumulating houses, and boyfriends, and dogs. Buddhism is not about being better than everyone else, or teaching them you're the boss, or showing them a thing or two. It is not about creating beautiful and wonderful things the way art is, but paradoxically it creates the most wonderful, beautiful thing I can think of. The artist is about himself, the prima donnas, the fast licks he can kick off his guitar, the grand master piece that sits at the Tate Gallery, that's what the artist seeks. Fans, money, flashing lights, recognition among Manhattan bankers for that two billion-dollar painting you sold, that's what he seeks. What does a Buddha seek? Nothing other than enlightenment. What does a Bodhisattva seek? The enlightenment of all beings. In a situation like that there is not much room for what the artist wants.

Art seeks to sell what is transitory as permanent. Buddhism first of all is not really selling something, but I think if it were to sell something it would sell nothingness. Buddhism according to some really does not even seek converts, although in some areas, mostly East Asia a little converting does occur. I believe the general assumption is that if one is meant to become enlightened it will happen by one means or the other. A casual acquaintance, a subtle introduction, something in one's life experience will lead one to the path.

By being so involved with the wonder and power of the art they create, artists dilute themselves. The art becomes more real than it is. The experience of seeing, or touching, or hearing, is more than what the senses are taking in. That is to say so much meaning is ascribed to the particular affect of the art that we are lead to believe that the art is more powerful or important than it is; or at least more so than a Buddha would see it as. The Buddha said "to hear is just hearing, to see is just seeing..." On the artist's side he would have us think "to hear my music is the world, to see my painting is bliss." This simply does not work from a Buddhism point of view.

At this point we can relay an experience our street musician had after a retreat he thinks to himself: "What in the world are all these silly things I worry about. That song, it means nothing, all the emotion, the angst, the pain, the fear; its all just a bunch of nonsense, it means nothing, it says nothing, it's junk, what am I doing. All those silly gigs, they don't mean anything, I haven't helped anyone, taught anyone, I have done nothing, nothing with my life, that's horrible! "

Chapter IV

The Street Musician Enters

The street musician enters our story when the musician realizes what he has been striving for is not real; he has been striving for something that is fundamentally not him. The process of Buddhism is one of losing all the unnecessary stuff we fill ourselves with. The day dreams, the greed, foolishness, and delusion are all slowly, layer by layer through the meditative and spiritual practices stripped away like the layers of an onion. Of course he is a musician, the tunes, the melancholy, and pure joy are there. No need to coax them out, to fake them, or create them. It is clear that he is a musician, while his spiritual training over the past few years has shown him clearly that his current lifestyle does not fulfill him, and leads him away from the path, in his heart and soul he IS a musician. Now if the time when he must come to some resolution of the two sides of his existence. On one side, he is a joker, a tune smith, a prima donna, and an angry youth; on the other he has realized the ridiculousness of all that society holds so dear, the vast quiet space of enlightenment, or morality, and the law of cause and effect. It is easy to compartmentalize one's life. Leaving the spiritual here, and secular there. It is only those who really believe in what they are doing, those who have "gone both sides of the circle" as in Christmas Humphrey's book, that realize to be on a true spiritual path is to realize the necessity is has for every part of their life. As in Humphrey's autobiography, the true spirit seeker does not expect all the answers to be right there for the grasping. We must tread seemingly backwards to get to where we belong. The Buddha did say that as we become true practitioners we will loose all interest in ceremony and ritual. We will no longer grasp the "religion" that saved us. However, the flip side of this is that we will integrate the practice into every second of our lives, and understand why things could not possibly be any different.

He realizes he cannot live a double life. Of course the musician's life is real in the day to day sense. Of course his life's accomplishments are real. Not only that playing on stage truly does make him happy in a sense, it fills him with joy and joyfulness equal to that of the Bodhisattva guiding millions of beings to enlightenment. But there is some discord in this life he has now, something he must change.

The Buddha is interpreted as having taught that we

have no soul; in some ways we are "no one". This "no one" is interpreted somewhat inaccurately sometimes. The issue of our street musician striving for something that is not real centers around this point. Sure, his seeking of gigs, and record contracts, and new tunes are real, but they don't last, and so are not as unchanging as other things; for example the Four Nobel Truths which have been true in every sense since the dawn of mankind. In the law there are "real" property, and all other property. The real property is the land, and those things attached to it, that land has been around much longer than any of us, and will last long after we are gone. This concept might help make some sense of the whole "no self" "no soul" concept. In short, the gigs are real, but looking at the big picture, as Buddhism tends to make a person do; the gigs don't really amount to much. As

Humphry Bogart's character in Casa Blanca said, in summary "The affairs of three people in this big world don't amount to a hill of beans." So, our musician finds himself wondering if there is "soul-lessness" then is he real in any way that matters. Is his life real, are the records real, is his career real? Of course they are. The Buddha did not teach that we are meaningless, nothings. On the contrary he taught that it is in the human existence that we are fortunate to be wise enough to grasp the Teachings and get the heck out of Samsara. Our musician has gone so high and accomplished so many things it is a real shock when he begins to question it. The massively important questions of "who am I, where am I"; those questions stuck in our consciousness since prehistoric times start to haunt him now.

The street musician seeks the peace of Nirvana; he has set his course, he can clearly see his goal, there is no going back. The music just puts up a smoke screen, it does nothing, and no longer means anything to him. In most cases what we do on a day to day basic is a smoke screen, the jobs, the family lives, the, this and that we do, they don't amount to a hill of beans either. He plays what the fans want to hear, or what gives him an ego boost, or what the recording companies will pay the most for, or what gives him that good feeling. Through his Zen practice he has learned it is all just foolishness. The silly gigs, the screaming fans; it means nothing.

Playing does not do it for him anymore, but still in his heart-of-hearts he IS a musician. What can he do? Where should he turn? On a fresh spring day, in cool and green England he finds himself with a few spare moments. He is taking a day off in London after a concert Saturday. Monday he flies to Brussels. The rest of the band is off doing whatever

298

it is they do on these trips. He stands at the window, overlooking Russell Square; they picked a small but quaint and discrete hotel. He thinks back to his childhood days, playing his six string among friends, playing the old tunes everyone would sing along with: the Beatles, John Denver, Bob Dylan; they all made sense. Those were good days, simple days. It's a nice afternoon, warm, gently warm late May, a good day to be outside. So he goes outside, his old acoustic six string in hand. He gets on the subway "the tube" as they call it. No manager, no band, no fans to be seen. He gets off at the
Black Friars and walks a short way to where he can get a bus connection to the southern side of the Black Friars Bridge, where he knows there is a tunnel showing historic scenes from London's past, it is illuminated with some somewhat dirty florescent lights, but it doesn't matter. He puts his guitar case to one side of the passage, gets out the guitar, and starts to play. He sings: "It's been a hard day's night..." It's subtle, no one really plays the Beatles anymore. He then goes on to John Denver, and some tunes of his own. He plays tunes from his childhood, the ones he really loves, the simple ones, the ones that speak to his heart. He plays the ones he wants, when he wants, how he wants. He does a few improvisations, some ideas he has been working on. No one recognizes him, people just pass by, on their

way to do this or that. Their steps echo in the passage way, with its dim lights, and the smell of spring in the air. Some smile,
some toss a coin or two in his case, some stop and listen awhile. He's a street musician, and he likes it.

Through this experience he has come to the single most important realization of his spiritual journey. Life is simple, people are complicated. His life as a rock star was just filled with one searching after the other. A search for money, fame, power, girls, drugs, you name it. There was no settled feeling, no peace. He was always "someone" always going "somewhere" to accomplish some all important thing. Jack Kornfield, one of the best Vippassana teachers in modern America wrote a book titled Being No One, Going No Where, this is really what the Buddhist practitioner must come to understand and on some level enjoy. It is of course much easier said than done. To just simply be, in this world of goals, and dreams, constant over-entertainment, all the electric wizzers and buzzers, the Las Vegas lights, the multinational corporations, the movie stars, and the sensationist new broadcasting. Where is one to find peace in all that? All the activity made it practically impossible for him to be no one.

He feels tired, down deep in his soul, weary as a

man who has laboured hard in the fields all day. He thinks to himself "it's been a hard day's night, yes it really has." He smiles to himself, thinking of all he has seen, all he has done. Does it really mean anything? Maybe not. All he really wanted to do was play the guitar. He just enjoyed playing. All the stage gymnastics, lights, sound effects, the tight leather pants; they didn't mean anything. He just wanted to touch people, to tell a tale that would connect with people, that would make them happy. He didn't want to play something because RCA would sign a deal with him, he didn't want to write a song because he could play it on seven continents; he just wanted to play some simple tunes he made up himself, that expressed who he is, and what he means in the world. "What has happened to all that?" He thinks. "Who have I become? I should be a street musician? Why not?"

Birth of the Street Musician

He must tell the band it is all over, his rock band days are over. They are a bit disappointed, but the average life span of a rock band these days is fairly short. They usually get into some trouble, but can retire all multi-millionaires, generally the public gets tired of bands after awhile, the average attention span of people is so short these days. The band's members spread over the earth's four corners, forming new bands, doing commercials, writing and being in motion pictures.

As for our street musician/Zen master, he is finally able to progress to the next step of his spiritual journey. He keeps on thinking to himself: "It has indeed been a very hard day's night." He doesn't have much responsibility, no children, no wife, so he starts a children's foundation, making education and opportunity available to those in the dirtiest, most forgotten slums of New York and Los Angeles. This Foundation is to be a foundation to the rest of his life. He feels a deep passion for the work it does. While he loves music, he realizes it is not everything. It is a great joy to the students, and a deeply enriching thing he can do for society, but at the same time he realizes the transitory nature of it. He does it out of kindness and a sense of his new outlook on life, but it is not the total embodiment of his new philosophy. He spends time serving the Foundation, but has time for other things as well. He continues to be a street
musician, going wherever the wind blows him. Few if any people recognize him, he does disguise himself slightly when he goes out, but still the street is the last place you would find a famous rock musician isn't it? But then again, there is a little lesson, maybe

302

he was not as famous as he thought, all that money, all those concerts, but still, not everyone loves rock n' roll: It's not the total center of the universe.

He has learned to be himself. This is the most important lesson of my little tale. He enjoys the riches his former life gave him, but he is free to fully engage in the new birth he has experienced. Time and time again, in a hundred different ways my own spiritual teachers have taught me this simple lesson: "Learn to know your self, master yourself, and everything else will fall neatly into place." Never could a more important truth be told. I believe it was Lao Tzu, one of the early Taoist teachers who wrote "It is the master who sleeps when he is tired and eats when he is hungry." He learns the joy of engaging in life. For a musician, engaging in life is playing how one's heart tells one to play, playing for the sheer joy of playing. As a street musician, he plays whatever his heart tells him to. There are no deadlines, no recording studios, no contracts, and no tour schedule. He is there in the moment, as all good Zen masters are. In
that particular moment, as an artist, everything in his being shows him what to play; and he does. He plays truly for the first time in his life, he plays from his inner being, from his heart, even I would say from his soul. In so doing, he becomes who he was meant

to be, at least on a simple level. Traditionally, for Buddhism the only "meant to be" is that we all are "meant to" become enlightened. Even at saying so I shutter, because saying some one is "meant to" become enlightened is not really a true way of expressing it. There is no one holding a club over your head and saying "you must become enlightened." It is just that for the Buddhist, that is our (the human race's) highest achievement. Without this we travel from life time to life time, as dumb as sheep, not knowing who we are, what we are doing, or where we are going.

Chapter V

What Does Buddhism Have to do With Life, and by the Way, What does Art Have to Do With Life?

Buddhism, as the Dalai Lama has rightfully said, "Is simple, people are complex." This is the odd thing in saying someone was born to become a street musician, or even born to become enlightened, at the end of the day we were born to live. We must question if there really is any destiny in life. Does Buddhism say we are to have a certain destiny? While it may seem easy enough to say we are to follow the Buddhist path, when it comes time to apply the path, it is far from easy. What could that imply for our Street Musician to be destined, or not so?

He has learned a great deal, and lived a great deal, but from time to time it's important to stop and make sure we are on the right path. It can be difficult. Now that he knows about Buddhism, and has questioned his life to that point, it's important to see what it all means in the greater context of things.

According to Buddhism, we are born to seek joy, to create a better world, to better ourselves. We are born to grab life by the throat and make of it what we can. Those who are wise realize the importance of the spiritual in our lives. They can seek any number of religions or spiritual paths. It is just that for me, and for our street musician that Buddhism makes the most sense. It is really based on logic, and morality, nothing more is needed. Faith of course helps, but is not needed, because our experience teaches us that the path is true. Morality and wisdom are at the heart of every spiritual tradition. Buddhism is free from many of the complexities that make a religion hard to accept. We are not told to believe in "sins" really, just cause and effect. There are no real miracles, just a course in observation, analysis, and discipline. We do not appease some super being in order to gain favour and get rewards, we simply get what we create by our countless actions and thoughts.

Our Street Musician has lived a life. But what has he learned at the end of it? Has he become enlightened? It's hard to say. No one really talks about being enlightened. I remembered when I was a monk that one thing my preceptor told me was that if someone goes around saying they're enlightened they most likely are not. So the point of our Street Musician's life is not if he is enlightened or not, but that he learned many of the important lessons that life has to offer. He is no longer a slave to what he though he was. He is free to live.

So is a Buddhist "supposed to" become enlightened? You might ask. Of course from a strict Buddhist point of view every human life is one destined to enlightenment. This, enlightenment that is, is where we get off, the last stop; that is if we choose the path, which most if not all Buddhists believe we are meant to. Enlightenment is not really about life the way music, art, food, or a good movie is. Enlightenment, and the path leading to it are beyond life. However, for those who choose the path the practices leading to enlightenment are absolutely necessary. Friends have said to me "music is life". Once upon a time I may have agreed, but after being fully engaged in Buddhist practice, I have to say music is really not necessarily "life". It does represent an expression of life, but is not really necessary to it. Or is it you may ask? Is it necessary for "a musician's" life. In other words, does a musician not really have a life without music? The answer must be yes. Buddhism teaches us a way out of suffering, this is one of the solid and unchanging teachings of Buddhism, regardless of sect, or country, or century. Music in a musician's life will satisfy some aspects of that person's life, but does not "make him whole". In a way I find this very sad, especially because I am a musician.

So all in all Buddhism is not really about life in its wholeness, nor is music, nor anything else. Buddhism teaches us not to fall into the pitfalls of life. That is the greatest and most useful aspect of it, hands down, no questions asked. Buddhism is not really about life in that it does not teach us how to fix 1957 Chevrolets, or how to bake a cake, or how to balance our accounts, or even how to have a good time.

So how can we make any sense of this? Life really does go on you see. Enlightenment is the main goal, but of course society would crumble if we all went out to become wandering spiritual teachers as the Buddha did. Often our "real lives" at least as common society thinks of them; i.e. the It just so happened that the historical Buddha needed an intensive course, it just so happened that his true calling was to find the path. So he had to do it the hard way, he had to leave all his worldly possessions, status, etc. Not everyone should really do that. We can have enlightened lawyers, tea salesmen, mechanics, etc. That makes the world go round. But doesn't that mean we have to live double lives?

Isn't that a paradox you ask? Didn't I write earlier that in Buddhism there is no play for the sake of play? Yes I did. The truth of being a musician, is that it is not play for the sake of play, but play for the sake of what a musician, in his heart-of-hearts is. He is not playing just to play, he is playing because it is who he is. It is his singular gift, that which he has to give the world. Two and a half thousand years ago the historical Buddha, Gautama Buddha set out to end his cycle of birth and death, to realize the key that all humanity must realize. That was his gift to the world. On a much more simple level, a musician's gift to the world is the gift of beautiful music.

Art is part of human life. It may not be necessary, like food, or water, or sleep, but there is an artistic side to most, if not all people. The issues is what does the art MEAN does it mean anything at the end of the day? I would argue that some art really does not do anything for us, or maybe it is that not all art means something to all people. Art does teach some people profound things. Really, many of these things are as profound as Buddhism teaches. Art can teach us to love, to enjoy the sensual aspects of our existence, to be proud, to be strong in the face of adversity, to be kind, to forgive. It can also teach us pain, fear, hate, disappointment, and a whole list of other things. Unfortunately a lot of these things are not really real in the Buddhist sense, that is they come and go, they live a conditioned existence. They don't hold the universe together in the way the teachings of great religious leaders do. However art, especially the

better stuff teaches us what it is to be human. What an incredible service that is! The pain and anguish, not to mention joy and triumph of Beethoven, the post-modern contempt and dissolution of Picasso, or the earthy liveness of British India as Rudyard Kipling depicted all teach us important human lessons; lessons we need.

Art teaches us how to be human. Being an accountant, or a banker, or a furniture maker doesn't teach us what life is. Art teaches us about emotions, it is for the most part based on emotions. We live in our emotions, which come from the mind/heart connection fundamental to Buddhism. The Buddha said "Everything is made of mind." Or, in other translations "The mind is the world." This is all true, but psychotherapists know that we are emotional beings. The Buddha did too, but he taught us to see through the smokescreen of the emotions, to see them as conditioned and passing things. The emotions are important in Buddhism though. Compassion, love, and also hate and aversion are very important. We don't live in the emotions though, they are a part of us, but they don't take over.

Art unfortunately relies on the emotions too much, making a mockery of the mind, the logical and analytical mind. That is the trap. Art can teach the heartless to love, the banker to feel, but it can also take those on the path to enlightenment and throw them lifetimes away from the goal. Art can make too much of all these crazy sensations, emotions, and "feelings" that we have. It makes them too real. What would Beethoven be if we all did not feel in sympathy those feelings he wish to portray just by hearing it? There would be no point would there? Or that amazing melancholy created by Miles Davis' "blue" period work? Emotionality is why art is different from other "life" things such as a really great pizza or a beautiful, nice house. The pizza and house teach us how to enjoy our senses, but not on the emotional level art does. Mahler symphonies are in part about the great emotional roller coaster ride of life, the blues about our sorrow and joys. How could we communicate these things without this art?

Conclusion

Art is dangerous, it leads us away from the path. In realizing this, the emptiness of what his life meant (the role of a rock star) our hero has gone into the street musician's life. He sees his former life rightly, as a waste, well not really a waste, but something that is devoid of meaning. The weird thing is that the street musician's life, if we analyse it in this way is also devoid of meaning. One of the major points of this tale is that in his particular case being a street musician enabled him to progress spiritually, and also allowed him to fulfill his most fundamental personality traits.

The meaninglessness of his activities is the "emptiness" or no soul concept, and conditioned reality that the Buddha taught. Everything is devoid of meaning in the end; it is only the meanings we force on things that mean anything to us. The only thing that his rock career means, ultimately is what he thinks it means, and it just so happens that now he doesn't really think that it means anything. Again to use the analogy to Jack Kornfield's book Being No One Going No Where the life of a rock musician is very much being someone and going somewhere.

In order to progress he had to leave all that. It just created smokescreens in his mind, making him tired, weary, and dead (spiritually, not physically). He had a role to play, certain things to do and not do. He had to be someone. As a result there was no opportunity for him "to just be" as they say in some spiritual traditions, or as the hippies did. Every person needs this time of relaxation in order to be able to do what he or she needs to do.

The life of a rock star always gave him something to grasp out for. The Buddha taught that the equanimous mind is fundamental for the enlightened. This mind is characterized by a lack of both grasping and pushing away. One just abides in the moment, with out a wish or care in the world. As a road musician there were plenty of goals, aims, thing to do, places to go, grasping, and pushing away. No real opportunity to just be still. It is in the stillness that the Buddha saw the truth, and in the stillness of a Sunday London morning, broken by a guitarist's chords that our street musician realized all the pressure, falseness, and foolishness of his life. It is in that moment he realized that he did not really get any satisfaction out of playing all those songs that just got people excited, that brought in the crowds, that paid the big record contracts. It all means nothing at the end of the day, it isn't him, and it isn't

music. It doesn't touch
the heart like John Denver, or speak solid truths like
Bob Dylan. Either does it touch his soul, does it
allow who he is to speak from the heart, and bring
joy and truth into the world. After all, he IS a
musician, a real musician. What does he need all that
Hollywood nonsense for? He was born to speak his
own truth, to bring joy into the world, to sing the
songs only he can sing.

This story is about life, art, and Buddhism. The main
question of course is, can and/or should all three
exist together. As an artist, a Buddhist, and someone
who is alive, I must say that all three, for me in
particular MUST exist side-by-side. Equally our
street musician has found that giving up his art, or
Buddhism would set him off on a very bad path. I
cannot really speak for the whole human population,
but I do believe that art is a necessary part of life. It
may not be a big part, we may not join rock bands,
or have studios, but every human needs some outlet
into something apart from our basic needs of shelter,
nutrition, and rest; furthermore, we need something
apart from spirituality, as important as that may be
for those on a spiritual path. We need something
that is not necessary, that is beautiful, or appeals to
our senses. Look at all the beautiful Buddhist art
throughout the world, or observe the beautiful

reverence during Buddhist ceremonies. For all the austerity, the physical restraints put on the monastics, there is still a great deal of art there.

As with the historical Buddha, it is only through giving up everything our street musician knew in the past that he could become what he was born to be. Only in the giving up that he won, only in the deciding to change, that he could enter a space of unchanging. Once he had started on the path, it was impossible for him to turn back. As with anyone on this path, he had to follow every turn and twist in the road, all the lessons had to be learned, all the deep profound realizations of every spiritual practitioner before him he had to realize. His particular conditions were different than everyone else though, he was born with an amazing musical gift, which was part of him, and had to come out in some shape or form. He also had the gift of accumulating vast and important merit in past lives. These situations set some amazingly strong Karmic forces into motion. Given these two factors, our street musician was fortunate enough to realize not only the Buddha's teachings, but also to realize and fulfill himself as a human being. It is not everyone that is so fortunate, but it is my sincere wish, dear readers that YOU can be as fortunate at our street musician.

May all beings be happy.

END